ON THE EDGE

Wrestling with God in depression

Peter Brice

For Margaret

Published by the Millstream Press
29 Beckmeadow Way, Mundesley,
Norwich, NR11 8LR
01263 721523

1995

ISBN 0 9527116 0 5

Printed by BD&H Printers, Norwich

CONTENTS

ON THE EDGE

INTRODUCTION

Jacob fled from the wrath of his brother Esau, whose birthright he had stolen, and he worked, married and prospered in a foreign land. Later he decided to return home, risking the vengeance of Esau. On the journey he met a man with whom he wrestled through the night. At daybreak the man struck Jacob, dislocating his hip, and asked to be released. Jacob refused unless the man blessed him. 'Your name shall no longer be Jacob but Israel, because you have striven with God and with mortals, and have prevailed.' Jacob called the place Peniel (the face of God), 'because,' he said, 'I have seen God face to face, yet my life is spared.' But he limped as he continued his journey (Genesis 32.22-32).

My experience lacks the clarity of Jacob's but I have been wrestling with God for many years, many of them blighted by five bouts of depressive illness. In the most recent bout I have begun to rid myself of my idols and to find a real God in the darkness.

Depression is a wretched experience. To be depressed is to be on the edge: on the dividing line between sanity and insanity, between the exercise of reason and the threat of overpowering emotion; on the precipice over a deeper pit of blackness, despair or even death; on the margins of a society that does not understand and is reluctant to employ those whom it sees as unstable or work-shy. But the edge also offers hope: the sharp edge that has wounded me also lances the boil of poison within and cuts a way through the ring fence which I had erected to protect myself but which restricted my growth. The breach in my defences becomes the threshold to a new and different life, in which the cutting edge of a deeper understanding and the leading edge of new-found courage bring me to the brink of new discovery, to the edge of arrival.

Another edge is important in this book, for I am torn between the urge to tell my story and the fear of exposing how vulnerable I am. When I began to find a new voice in writing a sort of poetry, I wrote a piece which I did not fully understand at the time but which now seems to express my dilemma:

The world is made of glass
as if my tangled emotions
the fear anger sadness despair
and those I cannot name
are open to view
in all their confusion
and ambivalence
yet contained in a vessel
of such fragility
that the slightest shock may shatter it
and scatter them to the four winds
to be carried hither and thither
like dead leaves

Can I bear the exposure
of my confused feelings
in the goldfish bowl?
Can I bear the shattering
which would scatter them?
Which is the better evil?
And do I have a choice?

The world is made of glass
as if there were nothing more substantial
than the delicate blue green of a Roman beaker

Knowing so few have survived the centuries
I dare not hold it
for fear it will shatter in my hands
But would I swap it
for the solid crudity of a mortarium?

The poem seems to make it clear that I have opted for more exposure and less privacy, and I am encouraged to pursue this line by the response which telling my story received in workshops on depressive illness for clergy in the Diocese of Norwich and in seminars at St George's Church, Colegate, Norwich. Revealing my vulnerability emboldened other men to share theirs, but men often feel unable to do so:

Men pretend that they act
upon the dictates of reason
which they hold superior to emotion
or even intuition
both
we say
the province of women
But if we know ourselves well
and if we are honest
we know that we are as driven by emotion
as any woman
we recognise that the wisdom of women
relies as much on reason
as on emotion or intuition
and we welcome the feminine
within our own personality
seeing the union of masculine and feminine
as our route to an integrated personality
But we find it hard

to stand against the macho image
of whatever form
and the Church has several
In the end we have to make a stand
because the macho man
denies and projects his femininity
onto females
or those he regards as wimps
and punishes women and wimps
for expressing his own feelings
seeing their protest
as emotional excess
Thus macho man deprives himself
of half his personality
rejects what his feelings and intuitions
add to his reason
and learning no wisdom
fails to apprehend
the mystery that is God

Women often talk about their feelings and by taking the risk of talking about mine I may in a small way help men to be more open about theirs. But it has not been easy: the first draft of this book fell into the trap of presenting the rather intellectual prose separately from the more emotional poetry. The less tidy arrangement which now mixes the two may reveal a real person struggling to integrate his personality and a more natural interplay of reason and emotion.

The risk of exposure is not only mine. My parents, my two sisters and my brother are bound up with me through genetic inheritance and shared experience. What I say about my part in that inheritance and experience inevitably casts some light on their parts. My parents and the younger of my two sisters, who feature most prominently, are beyond any hurt I may inflict, though some may feel hurt on their behalf. My brother died recently but is survived by his wife and children, and my older sister and her husband and children live on. Should I tell any of them what I had in mind or even let them read the typescript? I might then be vulnerable to family pressure to alter what I had written, because others would surely see it differently. It is not possible to arrive at a 'true' picture of our family, and what counts for the purposes of this book is how I perceived it. That is not to deny the reality of others' experience but merely to say that they must make sense of it for themselves. I shall be sorry if any living member of the family is hurt. I have not included any specific happening to the detriment of any living person, and I make no judgements about what any individual has done because I have not walked in their mocassins. If you think I am being disloyal or critical, please reserve your judgement to the end and remember that love requires above all that we are honest.

I write looking back over my life: my judgements about it are necessarily formed with the benefit of hindsight. But life is lived forwards, and we do not know how things will turn out: we cannot plan and we are not in control, except for very short stretches of the way. I have therefore tried to keep the poetry as it was written in the heat of psychotherapy except where change has been necessary to protect another's privacy or to correct grammatical errors: it is as it was, often raw and clumsy, but representing how I felt at the time.

The clergy workshops were collaborations of a new kind: my psychiatrist Bill Hughes, my psychotherapist Jean Clark, my wife Margaret and I used my experience as a sufferer to show what depressive illness is really like. Bill and Jean's expertise was set in the context of my experience of living with depression and Margaret's of caring for me through it, and we used some of the material generated as we tackled my depressive illness together. Together is an important word: recovery from depressive illness requires the collaborative efforts of a team. One member of the team was not present: Roger Burford was the GP who made the first diagnosis. He lent a perceptive ear to what Margaret and I said and to what we did not say. He knew, as did Jean, when it was time to call in Bill. Bill is a psychiatrist who restores one's faith in psychiatry and in humanity, and he has the rare ability to explain in understandable terms his extensive knowledge of the causes and course of the illness and of managing the drug therapy. Jean helped me to unravel the painful past which led to the habits of mind and action which overstressed my system, and she enabled me to put myself back together again. Margaret held me when desperate, encouraged me to take the next faltering step, taught me that I am loved despite the twisted logic which told me I was not. All four have been essential to my recovery and I owe them a profound debt of gratitude. I hope that each of them will know what a good job they have done when they recognise parts of their wisdom that I have made my own.

This book runs the same risks as the workshops. My experience is not typical. Every person's illness is different. For instance I think that men and women experience depression differently: men are perhaps more inclined to feel trapped and women to feel isolated. As Jean and Roger have often told me, I am very analytical: I want to know how and why. But it may be all right if someone does not wish to explore what it is that makes him or her vulnerable to depression: it may be far too painful, as it was for me in earlier episodes of depression. Drugs may correct the biochemistry or provide a crutch, so that we can get on with life as effectively as possible, until we find strength to work at unravelling the tangled experience which makes us vulnerable. So this is not another self-help book on depression designed to fit all cases - there are many of those on the shelves of good bookshops. It is a description of how I have sought God through the experience of depression.

Because I have wrestled with the Christian faith most of my life, I naturally use Christian language and images. I hope that those of other faiths may find something of value if they need to seek the God of many names in dark days of depression. Some Christians may be disturbed by my inability to accept some of the traditional doctrines of the Church and may even want to deny that I am a Christian. The history of Christianity has so accustomed us to define Christian faith in terms of orthodox doctrine (though we often disagree about what is orthodox!) that becoming a Christian seems to require that we believe it all from day one. Thus many Christians shrink from confessing that this or that belief does not seem true for them, but we cannot develop a relationship with God unless we are honest. Faith is not the body of doctrine that we accept: faith is the personal and individual journey through which we learn to experience and to trust God. The nature of our journey will condition the theology we use to talk about the God we encounter. Recently I have experienced God in the darkness of depression, and so I describe God in terms of that experience. Later experiences on my journey may alter the way I talk about God and more of the Church's doctrines may then come alive for me, but for now I must be honest about what is true for me.

There is also the risk that you may be distracted by sympathy you may feel for me, but this is not an exercise in self pity. I am putting myself on the line, because I want others to avoid the pain which I brought on myself by the maladaptions I made to my family circumstances, and because I want to say to all depressed people the words that most helped me: 'you are ill now, but you will get better, if you really want to.'

CHAPTER 1

LIVING THROUGH DEPRESSION

I knew I was exhausted. I had been sleeping very badly and I had digestive problems. The first doctor I saw in October 1986 sent me for tests and prescribed drugs which soothed my very irritable bowel. Perhaps I would soon be back on form. But by September 1987 I was finding it hard to cope at work: my energy seemed to pour away through the soles of my feet and I had to sit and wait for its return. I could not make decisions and simple problems seemed insoluble. I thought I was not pulling my weight and I felt guilty that I was letting my colleagues down. Sometimes I felt trapped and unable to escape, and my mind toyed with the idea of running the car into a tree. At other times I felt I was sinking into the mire, drowning under the weight of my responsibilities. I forgot things that I would normally remember and I had vacant spots in the middle of meetings and conversations. Though I put on a brave face for those around me at work, I could not raise myself out of the black mood which engulfed me. I was often in a state of acute anxiety and sometimes mounting agitation forced me to escape from wherever I was.

One such panic attack convinced me I needed help. I sought out a counsellor, Jean Clark, and another GP, Roger Burford, who diagnosed depression and laid me off work. Early in 1988 they suggested a psychiatrist, and Bill Hughes gave me my first glimmer of hope in months. He told me that depressive illness is a deficiency disease. Stress had destroyed some of the biochemical transmitters that link the nerves of the brain, so that they were making faulty connections and disrupting some of the automatic functions of my body like sleep, digestion, energy, and memory. It was my depressed brain chemistry that made it hard for me to function normally and caused the distorted thinking that told me all was hopeless and I would be better off dead. I clung to Bill's explanation. Like a new convert to Christianity who tells everyone about Jesus, I bored anyone who asked me how I was. But I still did not use the word depression. The relief was that I was not mad, but ill, and 'methinks I did protest too much.'

An explanation is not a solution. I still had an illness from which the principal of a sixth form college should not suffer. I knew that at least ten percent of adults suffer from a depressive illness at some time in their lives and that we need more openness if people are to gain a sympathetic understanding of depression. But previous experience suggested that telling my bosses and colleagues was risky. Roger wrote a true fiction on the certificate, and I hoped I would return to work before I needed to admit the true nature of my illness.

I did not know then how long it would be. If I had known my recovery would take years, I might have given up. I was glad to have Bill's drug therapy to prop up my battered biochemistry until it could mend itself, but I still hoped to get going again soon. I did get back to work in the summer of 1988 and enjoyed setting the college on a new course. It was a fruitful and creative term. By October I was doing better and Bill suggested that changing from the anti-depressant to lithium might stabilise my mood. Far from it! I reacted badly to the lithium, becoming locked in a very black mood. I had several 'brainstorms' in which I became very agitated. Bill once described it as having a sort of epileptic fit while conscious and he prescribed an anti-convulsant drug. I became very depressed, hardly talking except to Margaret who kept me from going totally off my head - and Bill rang me up every day for a fortnight when I was at my worst. It was a long time before I was on a more even keel.

All the time, since October 1987, I had been working with Jean. At first it seemed as if a dam had burst. I poured out my anguish and frustration, trying hard to analyse it but making little sense. Jean tried to stop me analysing and saying what I thought: 'How does it feel?' she would ask. I found that very hard. She lent me *The Inner World of Choice* by Frances Wickes, who quoted a woman who came to a moment of self discovery. One sentence leapt from the page:

'I knew I must be still and let the mood talk to me...'

Could I learn to be still and let my mood talk to me, black and frightening though it was? At about the same time I read TS Eliot's *Four Quartets* and the third section of *East Coker* picked up the same resonance:

'I said to my soul, be still and let the dark come upon you
Which shall be the darkness of God.'

I think this is the key to my recovery. Because the mood was so awful, my first instinct was to flee from it as I had before, but this time some deep part of me seemed to know that the only way to recovery was through: I had to stand and fight, to wrestle with the mood until I came to terms with whatever lay hidden within it. Finding the courage to let the dark come upon me was hard. Perhaps a small part of me knew that God was in the dark with me, even though I could not feel God's presence. I used a wooden carving of the Good Shepherd to comfort me, carrying it around with me and keeping it always within sight. I did not feel God, because the God I knew was an idol, implanted by my clerical family (how clergy children suffer for their parents' beliefs!) and by poor religious teaching in church and school.

Did I really let the dark come upon me? I seemed to have no choice, for the mood descended like a black cloud, but at some deep unconscious level I believe I did have a choice. I might have found a new challenge to bury the mood under a sea of adrenaline as I had often done before and as perhaps I almost did again in the summer term of 1988, but then I would have had some other stress-induced illness. Perhaps I knew this was my best chance of letting the dark come upon me: my daughters were more or less on their own feet, Margaret was stronger than she had ever been, and I had found a group of professionals whom I trusted. If I ducked it, I would go to my grave a damaged and incomplete person.

Yet letting the dark come upon me was dangerous. I had no plan to kill myself but I was troubled by suicidal thoughts. At times I had to fight a powerful urge to turn the car into a tree and sometimes I had to stop while I regained control of myself. At other times I had a strangling sensation round my neck: I felt it as a physical constriction as well as an impulsion to hang myself. These desperate feelings were very frightening, perhaps because I was afraid of dying and perhaps because I was aware that a brainstorm might push me into actions that later I would not be able to regret. The risk was real, for my sister Janet had died some fifteen years earlier from an overdose of drugs. For some weeks in late 1988 I was afraid to be left on my own, and Bill asked whether I would feel safer in hospital. It helped when Margaret, Roger, Jean and Bill took my thoughts of suicide seriously, and when Margaret asked me to promise that I would not intentionally take my life, though I have heard Samaritans say that this is not good policy because it adds more guilt to what is already a guilt-ridden situation. It was some months before I could say: 'I know I do not want to take my life.'

Being in the dark was indescribably painful. Margaret held me for hours at a time when I was at my worst, shaking and crying as I recovered from a brainstorm. At this stage Bill saw me once a week and Jean twice. They supported me while I let the dark come upon me, but I had to find my own way through the dark. Even if they had been on similar journeys they could not do my journeying through the dark for me. I had to do the work myself.

I found it hard to know what the work was. Quite often I thought 'if I can solve this problem, then I'll be all right.' But if I did solve it, there was usually another round the corner. I was very anxious, making mountains out of things that once would have been molehills. At this stage Bill lent me a good book on cognitive therapy which suggested talking back to this sort of distorted thinking. I took six weeks to read it and then felt guilty because I could not follow all its good suggestions. I half-joked with Bill that I would rewrite it in short readable sections, and that was the start of the collaboration which led us to the clergy workshops. But it was still largely brain work.

Jean wanted me to focus on my feelings and she asked me to write and draw without thinking about what came out. She wanted to release my imagination, to enable other parts of my personality to speak, to let the child within me to tell how it was. Working with some of Jean's pictures I found that child. At first she was a seven year old girl, puzzled and anxious, perhaps because the feminine in me, which now seems quite strong, had been suppressed through my fear of the uncontrolled women who dominated my early life. A session with Jean often gave rise to a scribble covered in her writing or mine. Then I began to draw on my own, at first rapidly in felt tip, ten pictures in one session, sixteen in another, but when I began to paint the rate slowed. I worked with great intensity, allowing no interruptions or questions. The pictures had to say what they would say without influence from others.

I was surprised at what emerged: the cancer which nearly killed my mother when I was seven and the fear around it which blocked the light; the aggression that the child in me (by then most definitely a boy!) felt towards my over-dominant father and my manipulative mother; the rage, not all of it mine, that threatened to blow my world apart. In picture I could explore my feelings and I began to see that my fear of the cancer and the rage was one of the roots of my black mood. Perhaps owning and facing the cancer and the rage might restore the light and renew my energy. The pictures developed their own mythology of a puritan and three witches: how apt in a clerical family.

Three paintings deserve especial mention. The first showed the black arcade of a church. In one arch my hands held a cauldron containing a poisonous brew over a raging fire. The puritan had become a dragon whose fiery breath fuelled the flames which burned the witches as they stirred their brew of rage, depression, jealousy and fear. By now a word-processor was enabling me to write more creatively and this is what I wrote about it:

The scales of the green-crested dragon glow red
as the white flame of his breath
revives the fire beneath the cauldron
The witches stir the bubbling brew
of green eyes and yellow livers
red tongues and black hearts
Boiling over
its foul infection
poisons and burns me
as I vainly try
to hold up the cauldron
lest it spill
on all who seek warmth at the fire

I wondered whether I could tip the contents of the cauldron into the fire and escaped from the burning. In the next arch I showed that happening, but only one third of the arch and of the event was shown. I seemed unconvinced that I could let go, but I was sure I could when in this extract from a later poem I addressed St George:

Kill the dragon
Burn the witches
Overturn the cauldron
Let the fire consume
the poisonous brew
Here is a worthy opponent
George

But I have no need of you
for the dragon's fire
and the witches' spell
only burn and poison
when I accept their magic
When I deny their power
the dragon becomes a dinosaur
the witches have no flame
to revive the fire
beneath the cauldron
and I can throw its contents
onto the dying flames myself

The second picture, painted on the reverse of the first, revealed that I had let go of the cauldron. The arcade of the first picture had become a beer cellar, curiously sited in the crypt of a church; the fiery rage was reduced and safely contained in a barrel; the witches and the puritan had gone, leaving only the ghosts of their hats and gowns; the scales of the dragon had become a staircase out of the cellar, from which I was about to emerge; through the door of the church I could see the yellow brick road winding across the meadow to the river past the flowers which had sprung from the shadowy crypt/cellar; a punt awaited me, so that I could punt up river in the light towards the welcoming and wise darkness of death. The clock in the church tower, like that at Granchester, stood at ten to three.

The third picture had its origin in dreams about snakes, dreams that had terrified me from childhood. The snakes I painted represented the tangled relationships in my childhood household, which caused me to be abused. Those involved would probably not have seen what happened as abuse and I lay no lay blame on anyone for actions which arose from their own sad pasts, but what emerged as Jean and I worked with this picture and the writing arising from it was that I felt abused. A recent conversation with my remaining and much older sister has confirmed the accuracy of my childhood perceptions. The picture still disturbs me but it represented a crucial stage in my recovery. Within it there was a rather weak image of a cat, which a dream transformed into one of power, and this is what I wrote about it:

The cat defends her territory
by a frontal assault
on the intruder
Aiming
with a fiercesome display
to drive the snake away
forever
she draws herself up
to more than her greatest height
and hurls herself at the snake
yowling and spitting
fur on end
claws and teeth flying
caring nothing for the snake's venom
or sinuous curling strength
Surprised by the fury of the attack
and not wishing to bite
unless its life is threatened

the snake turns tail
and flees

The cat stalks round her territory
as if to say
This is mine
Beware
those who trespass here
And then
adrenaline subsiding
she sleeps
one eye partially open
as if to say
Don't you dare return

The snake
being wise
remembers

Perhaps the cat symbolised the growing energy that was enabling me to come to terms with the past, to face its emotions and put them in their proper place, even if I still needed to be on guard against an ambush! I dream about snakes less often now, and when I do now some part of me knows even while I am in the dream that I need not be afraid.

Writing replaced drawing and painting. Most of it had value only for therapeutic reasons, enabling me to express some of the feeling round the events of my life: the grief that I could not feel at the time of my sister's self-inflicted death, the guilt that we had not done enough to save her, and the recognition that I had not forgiven her; the frustration of having a foster son who could not relate to me and my guilt when he was removed against our wishes; the grief when another foster son died after a brave fight against cystic fibrosis and the joy that he had given us so much; the guilt of colluding in the twisted games of our sick family; the negative emotions that the child in me felt towards my parents; the anger I felt because the church of my childhood had given me an idol instead of God and had taught me what I now see as false doctrine.

Much writing started from dreams that Jean elucidated without ever imposing an interpretation. She would ask what parts of me did the symbols in the dream represent. In the spring of 1992 I dreamed about a lumber room in which I hid wounded after two out of three of us were killed. Which parts of me had been killed off? Had I killed off the parents I had internalised as a child? Did it mean that, when my wounds had healed and I came out of the lumber room, Jean and I had finished our task? It was prophetic: we ended our work together in August 1992.

Early in my psychotherapy I wrote down three questions: what is my body saying no to; what is it that I do not want to acknowledge; and what is it that my conscious mind does not want to give up which my greater self knows I must? Jean and I had been tackling the first two, but while I was still seriously depressed I had to tackle the third: I had to decide about my future, even though we all knew that the decision should really wait until I was better. The Education Authority could not wait for ever: would I be back to work soon? How I wrestled with it! Would it be weak to give up my job or strong to admit that it had so changed since I accepted the post that I was no longer able or willing to do it? Would it be exploiting the system to take early retirement? Could I face an uncertain future? Would there be enough money? Would I ever work again? Unfairly, I asked Jean, at the end of a session when she had little time to respond, whether it would be immoral to use my illness as an escape. The vigour of her response, her outrage at the way I had phrased the question, lives with me still. She gave me no advice, but I knew then that there was an honourable door marked exit.

It was difficult to do. I filled in the forms and the reply came with uncharacteristic speed from the Department of Education. That was the easy bit. Telling my colleagues was hard. Going in to clear up was much harder, and on the last day I cried all the way home. I grieved for about two years and it took about that long for the cycle of educational life to work its way out of my system. In the year after my retirement I had several dreams about crashing trains which I came to interpret as confirming my decision:

Dreams
of crashing trains
point me away from the railway
without suggesting another destination
I must walk away
carrying whatever I can
abandoning what I must
to find a new and different way

The feeling of being in limbo, inhabiting the border country, being on the edge, feeling marginalised, however one describes it, is uncomfortable. We like to know where we stand but I don't, for though I am much better I am not yet fit for work. Yet amid the loneliness on the edge I have received some assurance and affirmation, for I know that letting the dark come upon me was the way to find light and warmth. Of that I am positive, as I try to say in these lines:

I am in a wilderness
a wild free place
saved from the shadow
of fear and tyranny
liberated from the guilt
which hides from the sun
and even from the moon
But the light has overcome the dark
and cast its shadows away

CHAPTER 2
FINDING MY OWN VOICE

I grew up with religious language ringing in my ears. The force of it was renewed for me in the midst of my depression when someone sent me a copy of my father's book *Saved and Sent*, written in 1939, two years before I was born. In it he paid tribute to the training in evangelism which Cliff College gave and still gives to many Methodists. The book resounds with the phrases of pre-war evangelical religion: conviction of sin, surrender to Christ, preaching for a decision, winning souls, Pentecostal experience, revival fire, and living on faith. It was the approved language which Cliff folk used and were expected to use. The language had a seductive power, almost making me think that I ought to be thinking, feeling and believing like that.

Although my father was changing his theological position by the time I became conscious of the language, he had lost none of his evangelical fervour: he was a most powerful preacher, in the pulpit and at the meal table! Yet even as a child I hesitated to go along with the language and the beliefs it encapsulated. I now judge that my early hesitation was right, because it is our own experience which is important, not whether it is expressed in the terms approved by powerful parents or preachers. We are right to resist the pressures - unconscious as well as conscious - to accept the received version of the truth, because it is a temptation which leads us away from the struggle to find our own words (or whatever other medium seems appropriate) to express the mysteries of our being, feeling, thinking, suffering and relating.

The more depressed I became the less meaning I found in the conventional language of the Christian faith:

Empty words
used skilfully
patterned in clever phrases
woven into powerful sentences
arranged in logical paragraphs
are still empty words
And all words are empty
when the hour calls
for different words

What were the different words I sought? I did not know. Because my upbringing and education fitted me to approach the problem logically, I began by looking critically at the language in which I had been accustomed to phrase my beliefs. I wrote the next four paragraphs very early in this episode of depression:

We stand a good chance of knowing what language means when we know the context in which it is used. Problems arise when the meaning of a word differs according to its context and we are not sure in what context it is being used. Drugs may mean pharmaceutical preparations in medical circles, a problem of dependency to social workers and a sign of moral degeneracy to some religious people. Misunderstandings may occur if we carry meaning from one context into another: it may be counter-productive for a moral judgement arising from religious belief to enter into the treatment of drug dependency by doctors. We need to know what language to use when. These problems are compounded when we translate from one language to another or move from one culture or time to another. So we need to understand as fully as we can the context in which the language is formed.

Our culture respects scientific statements because generally we believe that they can be verified by the use of our senses. If I say that my keys are on the hook, you can test my statement by looking or feeling. By saying my keys are on the hook, I also imply that they are not, say, in my pocket. If they were found in my pocket, my statement would be falsified. Scientists argue that if no way could be seen to falsify my statement, it would have no meaning as a statement of fact. A scientific theory may be regarded as provisionally proven when it has been verified by experiment and is capable of falsification but has not been falsified by contrary evidence. Verification and falsification are useful tools in language which deals with questions of 'how' and 'how it came to be', language rooted in our five senses.

So does language not rooted in our senses have no meaning? If we cannot verify or falsify the motives of a character in history, the quality of a poem or a painting, or the nature of a religious experience, does that mean that we cannot talk of such things in a meaningful way? For example, is all talk about God meaningless? God's existence cannot be verified in any scientific sense and it could be falsified only if believers would admit, say, that natural disasters and the suffering of innocents might count against God's existence, but such objections are usually explained away. So God's existence is not a scientific question: it does not belong to the language of 'how' or 'how it came to be', but to the language of 'why' and 'what for', the language of purpose and significance, where the meaning of the language lies in its function of telling us something about the people who use it and about how they view reality.

If we say that God exists despite the problem of suffering, we are making the same kind of judgement as we make when we trust an old friend despite some lapses in his recent behaviour: we are saying something about how we see part of reality (the existence of God) by analogy with the everyday experience of personal trust. So religious language may have meaning when it talks of that kind of experience which enables those who look at life through it to see pattern, purpose and meaning.

Even at the time all this seemed too intellectual, too heavy to lift my depressed spirits, but I could find no voice of my own other than the analytical and logical. Because I felt impelled to work out what I believed, I began to apply my analysis to the Apostles' Creed, perhaps the most accessible of the creeds through which Christians have traditionally expressed their beliefs. What kind of language was being used? Was it the language of verifiable and falsifiable fact such as science; the language of the probable interpretation of evidence such as history; the language of meaning, purpose and significance such as philosophy or theology; the language of educated judgement such as literature or art; or the language that grapples with life's mysteries such as poetry and myth?

Focusing first on what the creed says about Jesus, I passed over the statements which most historians, Christian or not, accept as broadly historical: that Jesus was 'born of Mary, suffered under Pontius Pilate, was crucified, died and was buried.' But how could 'conceived by the Holy Spirit' and 'virgin' be historical statements? The evidence was not good. Only Matthew and Luke cover the birth of Jesus. Luke does not describe Mary as virgin and virginity is not central to his tale. Why then is it central to Matthew's and what weight can be given to his evidence? He wants to show how the birth of Jesus fulfils Isaiah's prophecy: 'A virgin will conceive and bear a son, and he shall be called Emmanuel' (1.23 quoting Isaiah 7.14). He used the Septuagint, the Greek version of the Hebrew scriptures, which translated the Hebrew *almah*, a young woman, into the Greek *parthenos*, a virgin in the sense of *virgo intacta*. If the writer of

Isaiah had meant virgin he could have used the Hebrew *bethulah*. Could it be that Matthew's story of the virgin birth arose from a mistranslation?

Yet I did not want to believe that the stories of Jesus' birth were only legends, to be cast aside like Santa Claus as we grow up. For all my reservations about their historicity, the stories with the virgin birth, the angels and the star in the East still moved me. Were Matthew and Luke then the authors of a myth that we need, a myth that transcends the rational and speaks to the depth and fullness of our being about the intersection of the divine and the eternal with the human and the transient? And I began to appreciate how myth may express profound truth, truth beyond the scope of analytical language; to speak to our heart and our head, our emotion and our reason, our creative imagination and our analytical logic; to reach into the depths of our psyche and touch parts of which we are barely conscious; to evoke responses which to our surprise and delight change how we feel and how we act.

This brief discussion of the virgin birth may serve as an example of how I approached the creed. It was difficult to decide how much to take literally, how much symbolically or metaphorically, how much as history, how much as myth, and I found much disagreement among Christians. Might the context in which the Creed was written offer help? The historical context was uncertain: could it have been a test of orthodoxy like the Nicene Creed or the Thirty-Nine Articles? Certainly it came from an age less scrupulous than ours in differentiating fact from symbol and metaphor. So perhaps we could reasonably read it in the light of our understanding of language, as other ages had interpreted it according to their own preconceptions. But most of all I became convinced that attempts to define in words truths that transcend words may lead us to claim certainty where mystery is found or even tempt us into idolatry. We may avoid these dangers by accepting that many statements that seek to describe God and Jesus were and are couched in that language of metaphor and symbol which leaves their meaning open to doubt, and therefore to thought and faith. All human descriptions of God must be inadequate because we can only talk of God by analogy from our own situation.

As psychotherapy made greater demands on me, this analysis of language seemed less and less satisfactory, partly for intellectual reasons. First, scientists are now less sure of the objective truths of their discipline, for quantum physics and microbiology have introduced profound mystery and ambivalence at the heart of matter. Many of them take religion seriously and look for ways of talking to theologians, even if the benefits of this dialogue have yet to reach the people in the pew. Second, my argument assumed that language gives expression to what we think, whereas many now see language as a human improvisation which is ever-changing. Meaning and truth belong within the language and are inseparable from it. As language changes, meaning and truth change too, and those who control language have a good chance of controlling what is thought to be true. Perhaps that is why doctrinal debates are often about the language we use and why traditionalists insist that the old language is objective, rational and logical: it is hard to control metaphor, poetry and myth. Often it is language that gives us the building blocks of our thinking, the words, metaphors, definitions and concepts that we use to create a synthesis of ideas and beliefs which we call our own. The really creative thinkers, those on the leading edge of discovery, give us a new language.

So was I trying to breathe life into a religious language that was already dying? 'The holy catholic church, the communion of saints, the forgiveness of sins, the resurrection of the body, and the life everlasting' no longer carry the richness of meaning that they did to former generations, who believed in God above and man below, in heaven above and hell below, in a supernatural God who interfered in the working of the universe to reward the good and to punish the wicked. Such language seems to fit less well with a modern understanding of how the universe works. I felt the need for a new language to communicate the spirituality of which I was becoming aware in myself.

I found most help from those who made links between Christian spirituality and Jungian psychology, writers like Christopher Bryant,

Francis Dewar, Gerard Hughes, Peter Mullen and Scott Peck. Jung used metaphors that enable us to think about and work with the whole of our psyche. The ego, the consciously thinking part, may represent five percent of our being, the unconscious the other ninety-five percent. Within the unconscious there is a negative or shadow side, which has the capacity to do us and others harm if we deny its existence. The self is the fullness of our psyche, conscious and unconscious, which knows what is good for us, if we can hear it above the noisy demands of our conscious ego, when it speaks to us through dreams, daydreams, stories and 'Freudian' slips (see chapter 6). The self works to integrate every aspect of our personality, especially the shadow which it recognises as a source of moral choice and creative energy.

Jung's language seemed like a mirror image of Christian language. He has no direct substitute for God, though the collective unconscious echoes the Quaker belief that there is something of God in everyone. But if you substitute 'the shadow' for 'sin' in a Christian description of salvation, the parallel becomes striking, if you play around with the words, and the meaning may be greatly enhanced because 'the shadow' does not carry all the judgemental connotations of 'sin'. Discovering what our whole self really wants may lead us to what is right for us or what God wants for us: the voices arising from the depths of our psyche may be the guiding of the Spirit.

But the overwhelming reason why my analysis did not satisfy was that it only engaged my mind. Although I had begun to talk of the depths of our personality and of matters of the spirit, my emotions were not really involved. I read myth and poetry and talked about them: I did not write myth or poetry.

However suffering from depressive illness takes away some of the defences that our intellect normally erects around our emotions, the more so the deeper we fall into depression. All the experiences of our life are recorded in our unconscious and some will have aroused deep emotions - fear, rage, hatred, jealousy, guilt, anxiety - of which we are frightened or ashamed. So we try to hide them away, to repress them, but they will not remain hidden forever. By roundabout routes or in subtle disguises they return to haunt us, if only in our dreams. When in psychotherapy we begin to acknowledge them, feel and express them, we may begin to understand the past and in a real sense to transform it. Editing the tapes of our unconscious requires all our faculties, the intuitions of the right hand side of our brain as well as the logic of the left, the emotions and the intellect, and above all the imagination. To let the imagination loose we need a variety of tools: lots of talk, but also pen, pencil, felt-tip, paint, touch, dance, music, poetry, art, whatever creates a language able to express what is ours and ours alone.

I began with pictures, paintings or photographs created by others but which appealed to me, and then hesitantly and with little skill I started to draw in felt tip and then to paint. A mythological language emerged from the recesses of my unconscious, often through the medium of dreams (see chapter 1). Playing with these images enabled me to talk and write about how it was, how it is now and how I would like it to be.

Soon Jean's gentle prodding led me to conduct imaginary conversations with my dead father, and sometimes they became surprisingly and terrifyingly real, so real that I could feel his presence in the room. I was surprised by the vehemence of the feelings which began to emerge as I let the child in me speak. I was terrified by the rage which loomed up like a black cloud and threatened to explode. From an imaginary conversation of this sort emerged the first piece of writing which came from the hurting child within me:

Shut up, Daddy
Let me play
Don't worry me
Tell me the truth
Don't shut me out
Love me

Make jokes
Hold me
Let me be
I am my own person
I don't have to do what you want
You're wrong
Why not share the things you really believe in?
Why should I fulfil your dreams?

It was a rather ambivalent voice and still rather repressed, but it was a voice coming from a part of me that I had not acknowledged before. The word-processor enabled me to write as I had never done before, without thought for form or order, and I found myself writing prose in short lines, the poetry (if such it is) that you have already encountered. I did not always understand all that I wrote. The following poem, much further on in my psychotherapy, was a case in point. Ostensibly it was about a production of MacBeth, performed as a Greek tragedy by an all female cast. MacBeth and Banquo appeared masked and this is what I imagined the chorus might say if it were composed of wise women rather than witches:

All hail, MacBeth
that shalt be king hereafter

That shalt be king hereafter?

Do not listen
to the chorus of siren voices
which flatter your bravery
against enemies and traitors
which deem you worthy of kingship
They use your vaunting ambition

to lure you to destruction
These are not wise women
giving good counsel
out of that which is their own
These are wild women
out of control
in their fury at male power
They are witches
weaving evil spells from untamed emotion
to bring your doom and their revenge

Your instincts are right
Stay loyal to worthy kinsman Duncan
Your white mask conceals
the emotion of your woman's face
but not of your voice and hands
Stay true
to the milk of human kindness
within your unmanly breast
Confess your fear
of the feminine within
Do not throw your chaotic emotions
onto the witches
They will use them to destroy you
Do not listen
to your unsexed wife
poisoning your mind with gall
from her unwomanly breasts
She lies

Do not seize the dagger
that you see before you

Ignore the bell that sounds
the knell for Duncan
His blood on your hands
will be only the first you spill
to keep the crown that is not yours
Banquo
friend who knows too much
must die
and Malcolm and Donalbain
and MacDuff and many others

Double, double, toil and trouble
Fire burn and cauldron bubble

Out, damned spot
Your wife's inner being
unsexed as she pretends she is
knows water will not wash blood away
Unnatural deeds
do breed unnatural troubles
and untruths eat away the soul
bringing madness and death
The Queen is dead
unhappy King
who can
no more than his Queen
wash the blood from his hands

If you would be a happy man
knowing yourself for what you are
and loving what you know
you should not be king

Your mask lies
to others and yourself
You are not made for ruthless power
Terrifying your subjects
will not make you secure
but only increase the terror
of the frightened female child within
By masking her
you have learned to deceive yourself
allowing the witches and your wife
to collude with the deception
until Birnam Wood comes to Dunsinane

Lay on, MacDuff
and damned be him that first cries
'Hold, enough'

It is good
that you leave no son
to come into your poisoned inheritance
of emotion masked by grandiosity
and unwomanly breasts

The poem is much more than my response to a stimulating production. It uses the play to develop further my private mythology of witches and a puritan, which reflects much of what happened in our family. This mythology is personal, understood by myself, Margaret and Jean, and much of it must remain so, to protect the individuals symbolised within it. Yet there was much within it that I did not really understand until I came to face the feminine within (see chapter 7). It stands here as an example of what we all may do: to be healthy and integrated people we must balance the language of our intellect, which we may share with others, with the language that arises from the depths of our unconscious in the form of our personal mythology. Some of that mythology may resonate with elements in the great myths of humankind; occasionally we may write a myth that has a more universal application; but for the most part we are expressing that which is really ours and ours alone in our own unique language.

I can express my truth only in my own words
not in the language of yesteryear
nor in the language of Bible or creed
I have to live and write my own story
If it is to be a true story
I cannot take it secondhand from another source
however laudable or saintly it may be
I have to write my own scriptures
develop my own creed
I am a fool
not to use what others have learned
but plagiarism is no substitute
for creative writing
I may use the truths of others
but only to spur my reflection and contemplation
so that what issues forth is my truth
my creation and re-creation

So as the depression deepened and lengthened I came to rely less on the intellectual language of my upbringing and education and more on this new language which emerged from places I knew little about. I learned to trust the new perceptions which came to me, perceptions which had more to do with intuition and imagination than with intellect, more to do with wisdom than with knowledge.

CHAPTER 3

BECOMING MY OWN AUTHORITY

It is time for us to surrender
the male view of authority
as direction and obedience
deriving in some apostolic manner
from God himself
as if it were a something
to be handed on or down
True authority is personal
rising from the depths of our own being
where we commune with God
It is the only authority
to which I can give allegiance
because it precedes church or bible
or whatever else men call authority
I cannot do other than choose
in the depths of my being
what is authoritative for me
and so I am my own authority

Many church people may object to my conclusion, but I am convinced that recovery from depression depends upon our taking power away from the authority figures in our lives and replacing their authority with our own. People often confuse authority with power. If the king tells the queen and the queen tells the dairy maid, that is an exercise of power, not authority: the dairy maid obeys, because the king has the power to punish her. Democratic government is said to act with the authority of the people, but the governed experience that authority as power exercised by lawmakers, judges, policemen, tax collectors and administrators, who have the power to enforce their will. Because we usually experience authority in a top-down power model, we rarely experience true authority.

Indeed our earliest experiences concern the two people who hold most power over us - our parents. They have the size and strength to enforce their will, but for the most part it is their superior knowledge and reasoning power which ensures the success of this top-down power model. If parents use their power wisely for our good and know when and how to surrender it lovingly into our hands, we shall respect their authority as wise and loving people. If they use their power unwisely for selfish ends, over-dominate us or cling onto their power by unfair means such as moral blackmail, then we shall probably rebel if we are strong enough or subvert if not: we may fear them but we shall not respect them. All parents fail: all of us have experienced wise and unwise uses of parental power. What matters is the balance and the overall motive.

Unhappy experiences of parental power may make us resentful of anyone who stands in any sense in loco parentis. Because we may not understand what has happened to us, we may treat our children as we were treated: 'I had to do that for my parents when I was a kid and it never did me any harm...' But of course it did, rendering us unable to differentiate between power and authority, confusing our relationships with government, employers and church. If we are fortunate, our unhappy parental experience may make us think 'I won't do it like that', but even then we shall lack the good model we need when life pushes us towards the edge.

As a child I saw my father as a powerful mind and will with high expectations of his children. He was in some ways a disappointed man: in his eyes he had not achieved a status commensurate with his abilities. We children should make the best of ours to avoid later regret. So he was inordinately proud of our achievements and, however hard he tried, he could not hide his disappointment at our failures. We were all aware of his feelings. We felt pressured by the power of his wish that we should succeed, and the girls opted out of the race, to his eternal chagrin. We were overwhelmed by the power of his intellect and my brother chose a field of study that was not his. Why did I choose a field close to his? Why do I now work almost entirely in his field? Perhaps it was my rebellion, and I believe that it succeeded, but at too great a cost.

As psychotherapy helped me to understand my relationship with my father, I began to see how my feelings about him and about the Church were linked:

> *I will not have his dog-collar*
> *I will not be subservient to a church*
> *whose hypocrisy I despise*
> *whose beliefs I doubt*
> *and whose competence barely rises*
> *above the level of inefficiency*
> *I will not be subservient to him*
> *and if he will not accept me on my own terms*
> *I will beat him at his own game*
> *But I don't need to go on fighting him*
> *He is dead*
> *and his dog-collar is consumed in the flames*
> *melting like so much plastic*

A few months later I recognised the link as projection:

> *What do I really know?*
> *That the church speaks to me*

with the stern voice of my father
and in his authoritarian tone
That I must stand on the edge of the church
until I can undo that projection
until I can stand in my own right
secure in the authority
which comes from the depths of my being
not from him nor from the church

How might I undo that projection? I had already developed a logical, intellectual case against what I saw (and still see) as the Church's confusion of authority and power. When the Church talks of authority it usually means the exclusive power to tell us what God's will is on matters of faith and morals. What I wrote early in this depression came out of my history teaching:

Living in England in the 1520s you would have been very aware of the power of the Catholic Church, which baptised you, married you, absolved you from your sins, said or sang mass on your behalf, and buried you. Its archbishops and bishops sat in the House of Lords, which had much more power than today, and the Lord Chancellor, Henry VIII's chief minister, was the Cardinal Archbishop of York and Papal Legate Thomas Wolsey. The Church was very rich: it was the largest landowner in England, and you might have felt its power as landlord. One tenth of your annual produce was paid to the rector in tithes, and failure to pay would land you in a church court, which also dealt with wills, marriage, immorality, witchcraft and heresy. The Church could enforce its view of faith and morals: public disagreement might lead to a trial for heresy, and a refusal to recant after a guilty verdict could see you burned at the stake.

The Catholic Church's claim to this power rested, and still rests, on

Christ's promise to Peter: 'You are Peter, the Rock, and on this rock I will build my church, and the powers of death shall never conquer it. I will give you the keys of the kingdom of Heaven; what you forbid on earth shall be forbidden in heaven and what you allow on earth shall be allowed in heaven' (Matthew 16.18-19). From Peter Christ's authority was held to have descended from Pope to Pope. Succeeding Popes extended their claims until Boniface VIII(1294-1303) asserted in his bull Unam Sanctam (1302) that both temporal and spiritual power were vested in the Church, the temporal power was subject to the spiritual, and everyone's salvation depended on being subject to the Pope. No Pope could make these powers effective and the temporal powers of the Pope steadily declined, though the claim of universal spiritual authority was maintained and reinforced in 1870, when the first Vatican Council ruled that when the Pope speaks ex cathedra to define doctrine on faith or morals he is 'endowed with that infallibility with which the Redeemer has willed that his Church should be equipped.'

By the 1520s English people knew that Martin Luther had challenged the spiritual authority of the Pope in his Ninety-Five Theses of 1517. He had objected to the sale of pardons because they offended against the central tenet of his belief, justification by faith. Luther's interpretation of Romans 3.20-26 was that because we are sinful we can do nothing to justify ourselves in God's sight but that God's grace alone can restore us to a right relationship with him by offering forgiveness through Christ's death on the cross: all we need do is to accept God's grace in faith. Luther set this against what he said was the Catholic doctrine of justification by works, whereby we try to earn our salvation by keeping the moral law and accepting the benefits of the sacraments. He was not fair to the sophisticated theologians of the Catholic Church, but he may have been right about the superstitious beliefs held by many uneducated lay people and their under-educated priests.

Luther's protest against the Catholic Church rested on the authority of the Bible: the words of the Bible interpreted to believers by the Holy Spirit would reveal the will of God. Yet Protestantism succeeded only where rulers protected or promoted it for their own ends. Thus in the 1530s in England papal power was broken by Henry VIII and Parliament, who together established the Church of England and removed much of its wealth by dissolving the monasteries. Under Elizabeth the Church of England was given a Protestant statement of faith in the Thirty-Nine Articles of 1563. As the century grew older the principle of the individual interpretation of scripture led to the fragmentation of Protestantism into many different sects. So the Anglican Church laid less stress on the guidance of the Holy Spirit and more on the role of the Church in the interpretation of scripture; renewed interest in the apostolic succession (the belief that bishops derive their authority from the apostles in continuous succession by the laying on of hands in ordination); and made use of the law against Puritan sects.

Where the Reformation was successful it replaced the authority of the Catholic Church with the authority of the Bible, asserting that all doctrine necessary to salvation could be found in it or could be deduced from it. On the premise that the Bible is in a direct and simple way the word of God, evangelical Protestants constructed a tight, coherent and logical doctrinal system, which gave them a certainty as great as that of Catholic systematic theology. Ever since they have defended this system with the vigorous exercise of power against any who have threatened it by their opposition or dissent. The defence of evangelical Protestantism was at the heart of England's Civil War; and nineteenth century Evangelicals waged a war of words against Catholics, Anglo-Catholics, supporters of evolution and exponents of biblical criticism. That some evangelical Protestant churches still exercise such a strong discipline over their members may suggest that they may be less certain of the premise of biblical authority than might appear.

I had never accepted the view which was common until the rise of biblical criticism that the Bible spoke God's truth in a simple and direct way; nor the circular argument that the Bible has authority because it says it has, based on proof texts like 2 Timothy 3.16, which can only refer to the then existing Jewish scriptures and which the Revised English Bible (hereafter REB) suggests has a rather different meaning from the Authorised Version (AV) or even the Revised Standard Version (RSV). The history of the Reformation (and of other periods) suggests that it can hardly be God's will that human beings, whether writers of scripture or leaders of the Church, should be preserved from error: the catalogue of religious wars, persecutions and heresy trials points to the dangers of certainty.

So I needed a view of scripture which would enable me to take the Bible seriously. Reading biblical criticism led me to understand the human processes which brought the Bible into being: how the writers wrote in the idioms of Hebrew and Greek; how what they wrote was coloured and biased by their experience and contains mistakes; how those who edited original texts and those who chose what to include in the canon of scripture made selections which reflected their current preoccupations; how translation exposes the human nature of the Bible, in that a Hebrew or Greek word may have no exact equivalent in English or the English word may have connotations not present in the Hebrew or Greek; how we have to live with the limitations of human language and recognise that much of the Bible is determined by Hebrew and Greek language and thought forms.

I came to see that we can say, without fear or regret, that we have lost the key to some parts of the Bible (much of Revelation and some parts of the prophets); that we no longer need many rules of the Mosaic Law; that we no longer face Paul's dilemma over circumcision, and so on. More importantly I saw that some of the Bible contradicts the teaching of Jesus. It is hard to see him approving of the stoning of blasphemers (Leviticus 24.13-16), the barbaric treatment of captives (Numbers 31.15-18), the curses of Psalms 137.8-9 and 139.19-22, and even Paul's excessive worries about sin and guilt or his emphasis on sacrifice. So we should judge the Bible by Jesus, not Jesus by the Bible and be content that not all the words of the Bible are the words of God. Instead of being the word of God, the Bible points to the Word of God, the Logos or the meaning underlying creation, revealed to us in Jesus Christ. The Word of God is greater than its expression in the Bible.

There are great benefits in this view. We stand a much better chance finding that Word of God within the Bible, if we treat the Bible as a human document, written by people inspired by their relationship with God but conditioned by the mind-set of their time. We may then be able disentangle eternal truth from the text conditioned by a pre-scientific culture. We shall know that we have no option but to struggle with the difficulties of interpreting these ancient writings in the context of our present knowledge rather than assert that the Bible's authority overrides the discoveries of modern science, linguistics and philosophy. And thus we may be preserved from making the Bible into an idol. Idolatry is the worship of anything less than the whole, the image of God instead of God, a part of the truth rather than the whole truth. We see the Israelites' golden calf as an idol and side with Moses in his rejection of it (Exodus 32). With difficulty we may spot the idols of our daily lives such as wealth, status and security. Very rarely do we recognise our view of the Bible or the Church or our version of Christianity as an idol, but Jesus warns that it is the religious who are most vulnerable to the temptations of idolatry (Matthew 23). Idols are dangerous, because they cause our truth to ossify, prevent spiritual growth and close our minds to the leadings of God.

This is not to deny the authority of the Bible or the Church but to say that a new definition of authority is needed. By any standard of judgement, even the most critical, the Bible contains much inspired writing. Our criterion for judging its inspiration should not be its source, whether divine or human, but its effect: does it make us respond to its truth, its beauty and its goodness, for that is where its authority lies? We need to let it speak to our hearts and minds, and especially to hear Jesus as one who 'taught with a note of authority' (Matthew 7.29, Mark 1.22). The Greek word used for authority here is *exousia*, whose root means 'out of that which is one's own.' What Jesus said carried conviction because he understood the realities of human existence through his own wisdom and deep experience of joy and suffering, and we respond because we recognise that wisdom and experience. Likewise the authority of the Church lies in its collective wisdom and experience and not in any power it may claim over the hearts and minds of believers. Indeed the Suffering Servant laid down his power that we might find love and he expects us to lay down any power we may have over the minds and hearts of believers.

In the last resort authority lies in the truth when I come to recognise it as true. If I accept the authority of the Bible or the Church, I choose to accept that authority and I make that choice on the basis of what I judge to be true. So in a very real sense I am my own authority, and you are yours. It is better to accept that with honesty and humility than to evade responsibility by surrendering our will to another authority. We need not fear the inevitable accusations of subjectivity, because our responsibility is to the truth, and truth is demanding if we seek it diligently and prayerfully. In that search we shall be helped by the Bible and the Church, but I am right to doubt what both say if it does not seem true to me. I may miss a lot of truth, but it is not truth if I am not convinced in all my being that it is true for me. I cannot change what I believe to be true because another authority tells me I am wrong: I may be convinced by argument but never by authority, and I must resist the attempts at moral blackmail which have too often besmirched the preaching of the Church.

I need my experience to be received gently
to be affirmed and valued
because it is unique
because it is mine
Only then can I test it
against and alongside the deposit of faith
to judge for myself
whether it is life-enhancing
faith-building and love-creating
to learn for myself
whether it is of God
Whether it accords with the canons
of scripture or of the church
is of less moment

For much of my adult life I have stood on the edge of the Church because my experience has not been received gently: I have been assailed by authoritarian attempts to prove me wrong, urged to pray for faith and for forgivenness for my doubts, and even pitied because I cannot share the faith given by God to those who put their trust in Jesus. How sad it is when churches regard doubt as a problem: without the saving grace of doubt we may never come to a faith that is our own. If I repress my doubts, I shall become bigoted, and if I accept something on 'authority' without making it my own, I shall be dishonest. No, doubt is healthy and normal. Doubt should be celebrated, for it helps to keep believers humane and tolerant; it promotes healthy discussion and intellectual honesty; it enables believers to seek truth which is born out of experience and dialogue; it leads to a faith which promotes spiritual growth.

Faith is not a possession, a gift that enables us to believe what we would otherwise have difficulty in believing. Faith is a disposition of the mind, heart and will towards an open trust of life as essentially good and of love as the core of life's meaning. It involves a willingness to take the risks which open up possibilities of discovery, creation and re-creation. It sees that in every situation of suffering there is a creative possibility which may bring relief and for which it is prepared to search. It acknowledges the mysteries of life and is ready to explore them in the light of ancient truth and of new discoveries, confident that the light will not fail. It looks below the surface of events. It is ready to plumb the depths of the personality, to face the darkness within and to listen to the still small voice of wisdom which rises from those depths. It tolerates and embraces doubt. It welcomes its autonomy and is ready to accept responsibility for its decisions. Faith is a journey towards truth inspired by trust that the pilgrim road leads towards the promised land (Hebrews 11).

Faith is the realisation
that each of us has an inner wisdom
which knows what is best for us
and the struggle of faith is
to quieten the noise of our conscious minds
so that we can hear
the whisper of loving wisdom
which arises from the depths of our being
And that whisper may be the voice of God

But I have to do more than satisfy myself intellectually that the case for a re-definition of authority is sound, I have to live it. Have I in my own being become my own authority? Have I emancipated myself from the power of my father or of the Church? Have I been able to listen for the whisper that may be the voice of God? Three different pieces of later writing show that I have made some progress down the road. The first was written after months and months of agonising over my relationship with my father. I think what I wrote was true, though I have more recently discovered how powerful and how devious his hold over me can be.

I have let my father go
not only in death
but from the controlling centre
of my being
I have to work with his genes
some of which I still resent
but I can choose
what other parts of his inheritance
I wish to retain
I may always have to struggle
with the internalised father
but I recognise him more clearly now
I am learning to forgive him
for the misuse of his power

The second piece came after I had raged at what I saw as the iniquities of the Church and felt rather guilty. Had I overstated my case?

How expert the church is
at making us feel guilty
for disagreeing
but I am right to disagree
when church authority tries to silence me
however politely or kindly it is done
I may want to refine or reconsider my truth
in the light of what church people say and do
but I am right to assert that it is true for me
and perhaps for others of like mind

I am right to challenge
the straight-jacket of orthodoxy
from which the Spirit flies free

And the third piece came at a significant point on my journey. Clearly there was some way still to go, as must be the case on any journey, but there was hope in the waiting.

A voice from without
and within
urges me to walk alone
through the wilderness
crying perhaps
and eating locusts and wild honey
And I say
what shall I cry?
and there is
no clear answering voice
only the faintest murmur
wait
But I am so bad at waiting!

CHAPTER 4

TRUSTING MY OWN TRUTH

My truth is always provisional
open to doubt and never certain
never enshrined in unchanging forms
which slowly empty themselves of meaning
It is always seeking and journeying
always and only a part of truth
never claiming to be the truth
What is true for me now
may not be true for me tomorrow
and may never be true for you
But that does not make it less true
and it is my life-task
to live my truth

This is not how my father saw truth nor how many sections of the Church see it, but in the depths of depression I was keen to discover what was really true for me. I started by thinking about the nature of truth itself. Was there something which could be labelled the Truth which is true for all people everywhere for all time? Or was truth relative, changing with time and circumstance? And if truth is relative, what security could there be for one like myself, already anxious enough in the midst of depression? As before my first writing came from the logical, analytical part of me:

Through much of its history the Church has preached that there is one Truth, revealed by the Holy Spirit through the Church or the Bible; that the Truth alone can save us; that we must believe the Truth and suppress our doubting reason, for doubt is the temptation of the Devil; that we must be ready to make sacrifices in the fight against the enemies of the Truth such as heresy, the Devil or the Anti-Christ. This view of the Truth has left many sad legacies in history such as crusades, religious wars and heresy trials. These days many Christians, repenting of the Church's mistakes, seek common ground with other Christians and believers in other faiths. But some, feeling vulnerable to the challenges of modern science and philosophy and of other faiths, are tempted to take refuge in fundamentalism.

Fundamentalism is a defensive reaction common to many faiths under attack, which asserts that faith takes precedence over reason, orthodoxy over individual freedom and law over love. Maintaining orthodox belief and behaviour in the face of rational doubt and cultural change is more important than respect for the integrity of the individual believer and the demands of love. Often fundamentalism calls for a return to what is thought to be the pure religion practised in former times.

Fundamentalists regard the Truth they hold as different in kind from the truths of science and philosophy and refuse to accept the normal canons of argument and proof. So some Christian fundamentalists cling to the verbal inspiration of the Bible, despite all we now know about how the scriptures were written, chosen and handed down, about the changing meaning of language and the problems of translation. Some take pride in their literal belief in the creation stories in Genesis, despite all we know about geological time and biological evolution and about the nature and purpose of myth. Many with less literal beliefs risk falling into fundamentalism because they think and act as if their beliefs constitute the final truth for all people. Fundamentalists in many faiths are making converts. Converts see the sureness of fundamentalist faith as a rock in a sea of social and cultural change. Many are attracted by the kind of deal that fundamentalism offers: surrender your will and your mind and we promise you protection in this life and salvation for the next. You need not grapple with the mysteries of faith, for we will teach you the true doctrine, but you must toe the party line, for we discipline those who stray from the truth or the approved modes of behaviour: if they persist in error we expel them, ensuring that they will not be among the saved. Those we expel carry away the projected doubts of us all, so that we do not have to face the awkward questions of justice and suffering which life in this world presents. We can project our own bad feelings onto them, our enemies or the devil, so that we do not have to accept responsibility for what we do not like or cannot face within ourselves or in our community of faith. All we need do is to maintain the purity of the faith and to bring others to salvation, so that our faith is strengthened and God's rule extended. God looks after his own.

Although oversimplified this psychology rings true for many fundamentalist groups. Because the bargain is largely subconscious, it is hard to be aware of it: I did not realise that my wiser friends regarded my early evangelical faith as fundamentalist, for I thought of myself as being a proper Christian, certainly no fundamentalist. But the risks are there for all of us: we may unconsciously project the evil or doubt that we dare not acknowledge as our own and we may be tempted into the idolatry of saying that our truth is the whole or the real truth. Mature believers know that they have to struggle with the mysteries and paradoxes of faith, that ultimately they are uncertain of their ground, but that acting in faith is the only way to spiritual growth.

This analysis went some way towards satisfying my intellect but my emotions were in turmoil. I felt guilty. Was I labelling people? It is easier to say 'so and so is a fundamentalist and he or she is wrong' than to say 'so and so holds some fundamentalist views with which I disagree.' So we tend to attack the person rather than to express a different view and by attacking the person we create conflict. Labelling tends to treat people as less than human, so that unconsciously we can project what we do not like about ourselves onto them and then feel justified in berating them for it. Was I dealing with my own 'fundamentalist' views in this way? It is so easy to become self-righteous.

I was more disturbed by the rage surrounding such claims of certainty. At first it seemed to be my own rage, as a dream suggested:

They did not listen
They attacked
what I was trying to say
before I'd even said it
rejected what I'd written
before they'd even read it
I exploded in fury
I was beside myself
consumed with rage

Certainly I was angry at the fundamentalists I encountered in my dream. Fundamentalists do arouse the anger of those who do not accept their views. When sporting opponents do not follow the rules of the game, we get annoyed and accuse them of cheating: we expect the referee to intervene and to penalise them. When fundamentalists will not follow the rules of logical argument if the conclusions conflict with their orthodoxy, we are enraged, particularly if our right to differ is denied or if we need to defend ourselves against intrusive evangelism. But there was more to it:

The rage stays with me
hours after I have woken
It is there
in the churning of my gut
in the compression of my brain
in the frowning of my face
I cannot rid myself of it
I have not chosen
this burden of rage
It has chosen me
as though it is the rage
of someone else
as if someone else
has heaped their rage on me
and I have no choice
but to carry it
however unwillingly

Did some of the rage belong to the fundamentalists in my dream? Fundamentalists are often angry people, perhaps because at a subconscious level they are aware of the fragility of their belief system. The anger is dressed up as God's righteous anger at sin - though the parable of Jonah and the whale warns us against being angry on God's behalf. Their anger may be aroused when others insist on their right of independent thought and judgement. Western Christians may understand how a non-Muslim minority fears for its human rights when a Muslim majority seeks to enforce Islamic law, but the same western Christians may find it hard to spot when a Christian majority fails to respect the human rights of a Muslim minority. It is hard for all of us, when we honestly believe that we are expressing the will of God, to recognise and respect the rights of those who conscientiously hold contrary views, and we may be tempted to brush them aside as the opponents of God.

But in the end I concluded that most of the rage belonged to the child in me, who seemed angry at the unfairness of life, in this case at feeling obliged to carry the angers of the family:

Am I expressing
the rage imprisoned
within my family's twisted history?
I cannot pass it back
to the actors on that uneven stage
Must I then accept it as my own?
Understanding
I cannot shake its dust from my feet
can I find some other way
to transform its destructive power
into creativity?

At the time I could not use the anger creatively, because I thought that anger was wrong - back to the problem of guilt – and because I feared that it might overwhelm me. But I was aware of how anger on all sides prevents effective dialogue between fundamentalists and those who cannot accept their views. It creates conflict among Christians and between Christians and believers of other faiths, so that we seem to be on the brink of a new age of religious intolerance and persecution. How can we find ways of admitting that we may be wrong and other people may be right - or at least entitled to hold their views without undue interference on our part? We are sure to fail if we assert that Christianity holds an unchanging Truth which is forever true for everyone everywhere. Are there other views of truth consistent with Christian belief?

I was attracted by the views of liberal Christians who believe that the Truth exists but is evident only in part, as Paul suggests in 1 Corinthians 13.12: 'At present we see only puzzling reflections in a mirror, but one day we shall see face to face. My knowledge now is partial; then it will be whole, like God's knowledge of me.' So the religious quest becomes a search for that Truth, but there are many different roads which lead towards it. So within Christianity many strands of belief - evangelical, catholic, liberal, radical - contribute to our fuller apprehension of the Truth, to the growth of ecumenical feeling and action. Developing closer relationships with believers in other faiths fosters mutual learning and respect.

Liberal theologians seek to remove from Christianity those aspects of supernaturalism which are most at odds with modern science: they go back to the roots of the gospel to discover the real meaning and lay emphasis on myth as conveying a meaning deeper than words can explain. Some accuse them of exposing Christianity to a death of a thousand cuts by giving way a little here and conceding something else there. Yet liberal theology enables Christians to grapple with their doubts and solve some difficult problems, and it testifies that Christianity is a living and growing tradition, striving to meet the people of each generation where they are, claiming no monopoly of the Truth and welcoming a common exploration of it.

But I found myself most at home, at least on the nature of truth, with radical Christians who suggest that the Truth with a capital T - does not exist, but that truth is always provisional, always relative. Truth - without the capital T is a journey we make, not a fixed point from where we start, nor a destination at which we arrive. History seems to support this view: even though Christians from early times have declared that there is one Truth true for all time, that one Truth has shown marked degrees of change over time.

As a historian I was not surprised, for historians know that the questions for theology and philosophy change as cultures and societies change. They accept that for the most part each generation creates its own truth as it struggles to answer those questions, using the accumulated wisdom of the past but creating a new synthesis to meet the challenges of the present. Historians also accept that historical truth changes and develops: facts are no more than probable interpretations, destined to be reinterpreted as new lines of enquiry are suggested by the preoccupations of their own time and as new evidence comes to light. They know for instance that there cannot be one true and unchanging interpretation of the English Civil War (or the Puritan Revolution or the British Civil Wars). That is history's fascination. And perhaps the same is true in other fields: scientists seem to say that their research results are only provisional and that today's working hypothesis may be modified or replaced tomorrow, just as Newton's laws of motion were revised by Eistein's theory of relativity and quantum physics is now causing us to reassess much of 'traditional' physics.

How might my beliefs be affected if I accepted that truth is relative? There could be no final and certain test of Christian orthodoxy; goodness could no longer be rewarded or wickedness punished on the authority of rules laid down for all time by God; and even our concept of God might not be a fixed point of departure or a final destination. Many Christians, fearful of what may follow, react violently or at least draw back from the idea that truth is relative. Need they be so fearful?

To test this out, I decided to look at how the relativity of truth might affect morality. It was not radical theology but Jesus who overthrew the rule book and the calculus of right and wrong as the basis of moral behaviour, for rules make pharisees of us all. Instead he gave the two commands 'Love the Lord your God...' and 'Love your neighbour as yourself' (eg Matthew 22.34-40), and he explained 'love your neighbour as yourself' by telling the parable of the good Samaritan (Luke 10.25-

37). He replaced the negatives of most moral codes with a positive: we are asked to do, not to refrain from doing. And what counts is the attitude of mind or the motive which lies behind what we do. Love is the central value by which we are to judge our actions. Love cannot be fossilised into a code of morality, for love is no respecter of rules. This is good, for most moral systems are culturally determined and change as the course of history moves on, posing new moral dilemmas and rendering some old ones meaningless. We now struggle with the consequences of nuclear fission and genetic engineering, but many of the hygiene laws of the Old Testament are simply irrelevant.

Accepting the relativity of moral standards and putting love first in our order of priorities (1 Corinthians 14.1) makes us responsible for setting our own standards. This has two benefits: we cannot use God, Church or Bible to 'blackmail' people into what we judge to be good behaviour; and by becoming more responsible for our own behaviour we may become fuller, freer and more integrated people. This is not an easy way, for it may be hard to know what love demands of us. The word Jesus used for love comes to us as the Greek *agape*, that love which makes us aware how precious (rather than how pleasurable) is our beloved (our neighbour) and which is ready to work for his or her best interests as if they were our own. Sometimes *agape* demands that after prayerful consideration we break the agreed rules of our society or of the Church, and that causes pain, as many whom we now call saints found in their day. And if we have chosen our moral pathway in fear and trembling we are less likely to be self-satisfied or self-righteous than if we feel we are fulfilling all that the rule book tells us.

So in the same way that we choose our own authority, we choose our own value system and moral rules, but to make a real choice we have to free ourselves from the conditioning of childhood. As I began to write more freely I began to move from the intellectual sphere to the realm of feeling:

Parents have awesome authority
They tell me what is right and wrong
Yet by their actions they confuse
the right and wrong
they so clearly distinguish in their words
In word and action they convince me
that I am guilty
I should take the blame
I should not be angry
I should not be sexy
I should fear for my soul

To rid myself of that burden was a struggle, but finally I found ways of using the anger I felt as energy for change. The key was my recognition that it is all right to be angry. It is better to express our anger than to bottle it up. Keeping the lid on may cause us to turn our anger on ourselves, bringing all kinds of ills, not least depression; or it may build up pressure until there is an explosion at some inappropriate time in the face of someone who does not deserve it. We need safe ways of expressing our anger, if possible to those who have caused it. Good theory, but the angry child in me needs much reassurance:

Don't be frightened of your anger
Peter aged six
Don't worry that your rage will destroy
those who have betrayed your trust
who should have made you feel safe enough
to explore your maleness
and her femaleness
to lead you gradually
into an understanding of human sexuality
in all its creativity

passion and joy
Your anger may destroy
what is negative in your parents
It cannot destroy their love
Anger can be the fire
which forges the bonds of love
Anger can be the energy
which enables you to transcend
their legacy of fear and guilt
Even if they did not intend
or you misunderstood
what you saw or heard
your feelings of anger are real
and need to be acknowledged
It is all right to be angry
I affirm you in your anger
You can feel and express it
knowing you are safe with me

Slowly the energy derived from my anger enabled me to make my own choices at a level deeper than the intellect. Being free to make my choices made me more willing to let others make theirs. The only valid criterion for judging between my choices and theirs is love. Jesus said: 'You will recognise them by their fruit' (Matthew 7.15-20, Luke 6.43-45), and the fruits of the Spirit, the things that are in accord with the will of a loving God or with what our deepest wisdom knows are good for us, are 'love, joy, peace, patience, kindness, goodness, fidelity, gentleness and self-control (Galatians 5.22-23).

So the relativity of truth has great benefits, though making judgements about what is true may seem harder. Words do not come easily when I try to give voice to what comes from deep within my self. When I have to make sense of the competing claims of rival authorities and of a mass of information, I am sometimes tempted to surrender to an external authority which offers certainty. But ultimately such a surrender could not satisfy me because it would not grow from the roots of my being: I would find the the bird of truth had flown from this cage of another's making. Persisting in the creative struggle for personal truth brings a real possession, a truth to live by, a truth of the heart as well of the mind.

No, no, no
churchmen cry
there lies the road
to chaos and disorder

No, no, no
I reply
Chaos and disorder arise
from the completing claims of men
to hold the only true authority
Down with orthodoxy
It is damnable
Up with heresy
It is the way to truth

Christianity has fragmented into hundreds of churches, denominations and sects: no absolute truth exists as a test of orthodoxy and a basis for unity. We have to agree to differ, and probably to accept that there are as many truths as there are people. My truth will thus be one among many, but the diversity is a rich source of personal growth. To serve me well my truth must be tried and tested, to be forged and reforged in dialogue with my greater self and with others. If I offer my beliefs to others, without attempting to impose them, I can hear how they sound and may modify them to take account of their views. I should be as gentle with the beliefs of others as I wish them to be with mine, seeking not to oppose them forcefully with energy derived from the rage I have buried all these years, but to listen and ponder before responding. The dialogue will work only if I am humble enough to believe that my truth is not necessarily superior: many Christians find that hard, but clearly individual salvation or the integration of the personality can be achieved through many other faiths. Jesus and other rabbis taught in parables to avoid the conflict which often arises out of debate.

I do not need to rage
on my own account
I do not need
to justify myself
to argue
that I am right
and they are wrong
I am not responsible
for what they think
for what they say or do

I am responsible
for myself
I speak and write
words of my own choosing
They need not listen
and if they attack my words
I can walk away
shaking their dust from my feet

To be true to myself
I must speak my truth
but I can speak it quietly
without worrying
whether they aqcept it or not

I can speak it
so that I can hear
whether it sounds true to me
and if it does
I can trust that some may hear
and respond with truth of their own
so that what is theirs
and what is mine
combines to make a greater whole

What matters is how my personal truth is reflected in the way I live: 'You will recognise them by their fruits.' Personal truth is not like knowledge with facts and proofs that we can master. It is a wisdom which grows through the medium of mind and heart, through the experience of living in light and dark, through the giving and receiving of love, through pondering and prayer, and through listening in the silence to the murmurings which arise from the depths of our being. 'The wisdom from above is in the first place pure; and then peace-loving, considerate, and open-minded; it is straight-forward, and sincere, rich in compassion and in the deeds of kindness that are its fruit' (James 3.17); and the Bible has much to say about wisdom (eg Proverbs 8-9, Wisdom of Solomon 6.12-21). What really counts is that our wisdom is grounded in love, as I once wrote for Margaret:

Only accept
what you yourself judge to be true
after you have opened
your mind and heart
to convincement by the truth
then speak your truth
with love
and act upon it in the same spirit

Others may not share your vision of the truth
but if you meet them in love
they will respect your integrity
and you may learn from each other

But I do believe Christians have a gospel to share. John Robinson once (in *The Roots of a Radical*) expounded Ephesians 3.7-10, suggesting that the gospel is 'hidden'; the riches of Christ are 'unfathomable' or in the Greek 'not to be tracked out'; and the wisdom of God is 'multi-faceted' or 'like a diamond shining in different lights'.

It is well that the gospel is hidden, because we need to keep journeying towards it, searching out its depths. We need to be suspicious when people make it too simple and easy, for the most precious things are the deepest, most heartfelt. If we could possess it, we might find it had flown from our grasp, or we might make it an idol. Yet there is enough for each stage of life, and as we catch glimpses of it we are filled with joy, like the man who finds buried treasure or a pearl of great price (Matthew 13.44-46), the shepherd who finds a lost sheep or a woman who finds a lost coin (Luke 15.3-10). Sometimes it is only afterwards that we recognise that we have been in the presence of God or in communication with some mysterious and deep part of ourselves, like the disciples on the Emmaus Road (Luke 24.13-35). This haunting story speaks of a God hidden within the interaction of human beings.

The riches of Christ, in the teaching of Jesus, are such that there is always more to explore. The characteristic forms of his teaching are parable and paradox, which speak to the whole of our personality, to heart and mind, to unconscious and conscious. We cannot expect from those riches to make a map to serve us for all time - they are 'not to be tracked out.' No, we have to react and interact with them, so that we grow into the full stature of Christ (Ephesians 4.13). Development, growth and change are the lot of those who would follow Jesus.

The wisdom of God casts differing lights on the mysteries of life. We shall never fully explain those mysteries, but we can live more at ease with them, if we allow the wisdom which arises from the depths of our being to enter into dialogue with truths ancient and modern, with the truths of Christianity and of other religions. In that way we catch reflections from the diamond shining in different lights, for the wisdom of God is not confined to the Bible or the Church. In that dialogue we find revelations of a deeper truth than the mind can apprehend, which will indeed set us free (John 8.31-32).

We need a gospel for today
in the language which we use
a gospel which speaks
to our minds and our hearts
addressing the doubts
we honestly and properly hold
recognising
that the gospel for me will differ
from the gospel for you
because you and I are different
and my truth is as true for me
as your truth is true for you
not expecting
that everyone can
or should
conform to the same truth

CHAPTER 5

DEPOSING THE IDOLS

Years of intellectual struggle convince me that we cannot prove whether or not God exists. The classic proofs are flawed. We cannot know God through the exercise of our five senses or through the arguments of theologians, philosophers, or scientists, however useful those arguments may be in anchoring our belief in God in reality. Our language lacks the logical tools to tackle the question (see chapter 2). If God exists, God is not an objective fact, a part of the universe, which science can investigate or philosophy define. God is mystery, beyond the human mind to grasp and beyond human language to describe. How could I apprehend such mystery without reducing it to my terms and so creating an idol?

Second Isaiah (Isaiah 40-55) asks 'What likeness will you find for God or what form to resemble his?' (40.18). He rejects physical representations (eg 44.9-20) but offers a host of similes and metaphors drawn from human experience but pointing beyond it towards the nature and activity of God. Sometimes the comparison is direct: 'Like a shepherd he will tend his flock' (40.11). More often it is implied: 'Who has measured the waters of the sea in the hollow of his hand ... ?' (40.12). The richness of Second Isaiah's metaphorical language is intended to fire our imagination and make us respond to a living God. But as yet I knew no such God.

Despite Second Isaiah I had difficulties with the image of God presented by the Bible, for science seemed to be leaving less and less room for a supernatural power who sustains the universe, whose actions can alter the physical circumstances of our daily lives. Had humankind created such a God to explain things which were once beyond explanation? Yet I wanted to take God seriously and at first I found it easier to live with metaphors that pointed to an immanent God, a God who dwells within the creation, a God whom we may find in the depths of our being or - if you like the Jungian language - in our greater self, or even in the collective self. But I also sensed that God is also different and separate from us. What metaphors might do justice to the paradox that God is both within and beyond the universe?

When depression made it hard to involve myself in a church service, I would analyse the words of the liturgy and I was surprised at how few metaphors we use to address God: lord, king and father are the most common nouns and almighty, heavenly and holy the most common adjectives. These conveyed images of power - and male power at that - and I wondered how my perception of God would change if I tried to avoid these titles. I found it hard to replace them because, although the Bible has many alternatives, they are not hallowed by tradition and familiarity, and when caught up in emotion I would revert to the familiar titles, as a poem later in this chapter proves. Yet trying to avoid those six words did alter how I thought about God.

Giving up images of an almighty king who can alter the laws of the universe at will enabled me to live more at ease with the problem of suffering: a God at the depth of our being is at least in it with us, and we are spared the uncomfortable belief that God could prevent innocent and unnecessary suffering but chooses not to (see chapter 13). Knowing that God would not answer my prayers by changing the natural law challenged me to find new ways of praying, so that my prayers rang less hollow. Some might say that prayer is then useless, but that is not true, for we are coming to understand, as pre-scientific healers did, that there are energies deep within us which can bring healing or acceptance of what must be. Prayer is one of the release mechanisms for those energies (see chapter 15).

I was also relieved to abandon the two-world view to which belief in heaven commits many people. The Christian task is to make God's love real for all humankind, so that all may have life and have it in all its fullness (John 10.10). Christians might devote more energy to that task if they saw the world in which they live as the real world. The 'other world' of so much Christian imagery might be seen as a metaphor for the ideal to which this real world of ours should aspire. Christian hope might then be extended to this world, not deferred to the next, and eternal life sought in the here and now, in the eternal quality of the present moment (see chapter 10).

Returning to Second Isaiah I began to interpret biblical language in ways which did not commit me to belief in a holy lord, a heavenly king or an almighty father. These analogies and metaphors were designed to open windows into the being of God. The idea of God's transcendent power may have arisen from people's feelings of insignificance and fear in the face of the unpredictable power of nature, of wonder at the beauty of nature, of puzzlement at the mystery which lies behind our existence within nature. If so, it is a good and useful myth, sometimes very beautifully expressed (eg Job 38-39), but we might want to rewrite it in language and symbols more suited to what we know from the explorations of science. The wonder and the mystery are perhaps greater than they were, for our universe is infinitely greater and matter so much more minutely understood, and we have reason to be even more wary of the power that can be unleashed.

Work on these lines might offer solutions to my intellectual difficulties, but the onset of my depressive illness revealed that my real problems with God were less in the mind than in my unconscious. Soon after I began psychotherapy I did a piece of free writing about my father.

I had been sorting out some of the papers he left to me, including the manuscripts of several books. I did some relaxation exercises as I tried to empty my mind and then wrote this at great speed:

So I've done the history bit. I can write a biographical sketch from the notes made on the papers. It is in many ways a remarkable story of real achievement: illiterate mine boy to first class degree and doctorate, many books and much acclaim. Yet in a sense he was disappointed. He felt he was unfairly treated by Methodism and in some ways that blighted his career. I wonder whether I share the reverence many felt for my father. Will anyone publish the manuscripts he has left? How will I feel if they do or if they don't. I'll feel a certain pride for him and for my mother, but will I feel a reinforcement of his hold on me? I admire his knowledge but resent his didactic, dogmatic use of it, and perhaps I resent it because I feel obliged to fulfil his aspirations for me. It was only rarely that he came down from his lofty pinnacle. No wonder I can't find God.

I was not talking or thinking about God and yet this last sentence came tumbling out. Words blurted out like these may be trusted, for our unconscious has probably slipped them past the guard of our censoring super-ego. A little later, using a similar process, I came to write about the childhood image of God that I had long since suppressed:

In childhood I saw God as a punisher of wrong-doing. He set the rules, I didn't keep them and I feared retribution. I had no concept of God as love. God was a stern authoritarian disciplinarian.

It seemed that I had formed a punitive and judging image of God from my childhood relationship with my father. His total absorption in his work made his infrequent but powerful interventions in family life seem like authority from on high to the small child that I was. Perhaps I gave him god-like status and muddled up his injunctions and my failure to obey them with my first ideas of God. Maybe I had projected my fears and guilts onto God and created the image of an angry God. It fitted well with the distant and righteous God of my Sunday school, derived from a rather selective reading of the Old Testament which emphasised God's holiness and commandments. God was the Holy One of Israel, before whom like the clay in the potter's hands I had no rights (Jeremiah 18.1-10) and who would judge and punish me. My reading of Second Isaiah gave me other images of God as a caring redeemer who knew and loved me (43.1-7), but they had not penetrated the depths of my being.

Looking anew at the teaching of Jesus changed how I saw God (see chapter 11). The New Testament testifies that Jesus is the Word of God, the logos or God's self-expression in the form of a human being (John 1.1-18), and Emmanuel or 'God with us' (Matthew 1.23). However we interpret the doctrine of the Incarnation, the central point is that God is revealed to us in the life of Jesus, both in what he said and what he did. God shares our humanity, our joys and sorrows, our good and evil. God invites everyone into his presence: the word 'come' is never far from Jesus' lips (eg Matthew 11.28-30). God goes out to seek and to save those who are lost: Jesus speaks of himself as the good shepherd (John 10.11-16) and tells the moving parable of the lost sheep (Luke 15.1-7). God forgives: the parable of the prodigal son speaks eloquently of God as a father who runs out to meet the returning, repenting son (Luke 15.11-32). In Gethsemane Jesus calls God *Abba*, an Aramaic word which is the familiar form of father, daddy perhaps (Mark 14.36), and we are encouraged to do the same in Romans 8.15 and Galatians 4.6. And the First Letter of John makes the identification of God with love (4.7-21).

It is God who calls you
Whoever or whatever God may be
he
or she

is at the depths of your being
Because God must be better
than the best we know
God is love

People often find that love enables them to believe in God. If we have a happy childhood, we may learn to love ourselves by experiencing what it is to love and be loved by our parents, siblings and friends. Falling in love we may idealise our beloved and experience powerful sexual attraction, but we may also be amazed that someone loves us and find that as we give ourselves to the other in love we become more ourselves, receiving ourselves back as gift. It is a mystery, and we have to work with the mystery, and to work hard, if we are to build the creative intimacy of a love deep enough to sustain a lifelong marriage. Out of that love and sexual intimacy may come a humbling and joyful participation in the ordinary miracle of birth, and the child of our love releases the enormous power of parental love. From those protective instincts we have to let our offspring go free when the time is right, in one of the greatest acts of self-denial love ever calls upon us to make. Many lovers and most parents know something about *agape*, that love which perceives the needs of the other and meets them with as much energy as if they were their own, but no childhood is perfect, and so many of us need the source of loving which is the knowledge, the good news, that God loves us.

The moving hymn to love, to *agape*, in 1 Corinthians 13 makes us aware of how far we fall short of Jesus' command to love our neighbour as we love ourselves; and if we are in any doubt, it is often easier, if we are honest, to see ourselves in the two who passed by on the other side rather than in the good Samaritan (Luke 10.25-37). And this sense of failure reinforced my childhood image of a God who punished me, who terrorised me as Jehovah terrorised the Israelites. I could see that this was not the God of Jesus but how could I rid myself of this idol from my childhood?

Discussions about God had often left me disturbed: perhaps I had offended the angry God who still inhabited my psyche and had power to punish me. The realisation that my feelings of disturbance were feelings of anger was a turning point: could I be angry that my father and the Church had given me a false image of God, an idol? One Good Friday I caught myself saying 'balderdash' out loud in the sermon and when I returned home my anger spilled out onto paper and found an unexpected resolution:

I am angry, Lord
Angry
that she dare preach
your wrath rather than your love
Angry
that she dare preach
that you did not answer
My God, my God, why have you forsaken me?
because Jesus had to suffer
your wrath at our sin
because he took upon himself
the just punishment
you demand for our sins

Lord, you must be angry
for you said
long since
I require mercy
not sacrifice
You must be angry
when we cannot see
that you love us

as we are
for what we are
Angry
when we project our anger onto you
and call it your wrath
Angry
when we project our guilt onto you
and call for your righteous
punishment of sinners
Angry
when by projecting them onto you
we avoid dealing with our anger and guilt
colluding with those who like
to punish and condemn

And yet you are not angry
for in your love
you accept our projections
and carry them on your cross
In your love
you offer forgiveness to all
In your love
you grieve
that many cannot accept
your free forgiveness
because they do not know their need
or want to earn your love

You offer your love to all
so that we may feel loved
and forgiven
and so feeling

may love ourselves
and others as ourselves
and be released by love
into love

As I put down my pen I was surprised at what I had written, not at my anger which caused me to begin writing but at the strong belief of the last two stanzas that God is not angry. I need no longer accept the idol that others had given me or that I had made for myself. If God was not angry, there was no anger to appease. I did not need to earn God's love: the parable of the prodigal son was true for me, even if I saw more of myself in the elder brother. God was not the father or mother whose love I must earn by achieving the success my father wished for me or by conforming to the ideals my mother had for me. God would not punish my failure by the withdrawal of love. Of course some of the old image still lurks within my psyche but when it catches me out I can expose it for the fraud that it is. So I am becoming more open to the love of the real God whom we can know through Jesus.

But other parts of my idol still remained. Though I had been striving to rid myself of patriarchal images of God, I still found myself harbouring a primitive image of God as male. My image of maleness was incomplete for I had not yet come to terms with the feminine within (see chapter 7), but working and worshipping with the Movement for the Ordination of Women introduced me to strong and caring women whose qualities put the lie to that strand of church tradition which sees women as occasions of sin and sources of temptation, as physically weak and emotionally vulnerable. These women were made in the image of God (Genesis 1.27, 5.1-2) and so within God must be comprehended their creativity, their self-sacrificing love, their inner strength and wisdom, their nurturing and healing skills. Where might I find metaphors to image the femininity of God?

The Bible offered limited help: wisdom is seen as feminine (eg

Proverbs 3.13-20, Ecclesiasticus 1.1-20); Jesus' adoption of the role of the Suffering Servant (Isaiah 52.13-53.12) places more emphasis on God's vulnerability and love and less on God's holiness and power; and he gave us a lovely feminine image in '0 Jerusalem, Jerusalem ... How often have I longed to gather your children, as a hen gathers her brood under her wings...' (Matthew 23.37-39, Luke 13.34). But that was not enough. Could I read the Gospel story in such a way as to image God in feminine ways? The Old Testament regulated slavery and the New Testament (eg Colossians 3.22, Philemon) took it for granted as if it were in God's plan, but we now believe that the abolition of slavery was right because slavery offends the dignity of human beings and so the will of God. We ignore the thread of slavery in the Bible. Could I do the same with male patriarchy, so that dignity might be restored to women made in the image of God? I could, by treating the Bible as the starting point for a tradition which remains alive because it is remade by each succeeding generation. Because language is ever-changing, we have to re-tell the story (as I have tried to re-tell the parable of the prodigal son in chapter 12), to remake the truth in our own words, to communicate our own experience of God. At the same time we have to accept that everyone's experience is different, for God is multi-faceted, like a diamond shining in different lights (see chapter 4). If we assume that our experience or the traditional experience of the church is the whole or the only true experience of God, we make an idol - and the Bible is very firm about idolatry (eg Exodus 20.4-5, Ezekiel 6.1-14, 1 Corinthians 10.14-22).

So the old images have value when they stimulate us to look for new, but if we guard them as the only true images, they will die on us. I enjoy the work of Janet Morley, Brian Wren and others who strive for new metaphors and analogies to illumine our apprehension of God. As individuals and as churches we may have to move by stages: finding feminine images to complement and soften the hard lines of the traditional masculine images and only then creating new images which enable us to speak of God without the overtones of gender. Some congregations, shocked by the use of feminine images, may seek to avoid the pain of giving up the familiar images and the hard work of creating the new. They may reject those who initiate change and support those who are distressed by feminine images, ignoring the feelings of the many women and men who now find some of the old images offensive. We should help those who are distressed, but not by agreeing that only the familiar images are acceptable. Churches need to find ways of freeing those who wish to explore new territory and of supporting those who wish to remain in the old, but few maintain a good balance of new and old, because they feel threatened by the wealth of symbols and metaphors needed to express a variety of experiences.

Yet if we are true to our own experience of God we may find, as I have begun to do, that love grows gradually and mysteriously in our hearts and the real God exists and is alive because he or she, she and he, is alive in us. God emerges from our dialogue with ourselves and with others and from our creative interpretation of the deposit of faith in scripture and liturgy, in myth, parable and poetry. God is the treasure we find within when we come to know something of our greater self, either by conversion - the sudden confronting of ourselves by the depth of our being - or by the dawning apprehension that there is more to us than our conscious ego, however much the ego may try to deny it. Some may never use the God language but may nevertheless have the experience of repentance or integration, while others, sadly, may be prevented by choice or circumstance from discovering that they are rooted and grounded in love.

God lives in the love that we receive, share and give. We know God because we feel God's spirit of love in our hearts and we meet God in the needs of other people, as the parable of the sheep and the goats suggests (Matthew 25.31-46). That does not mean to say that God is some romantic feeling, even if some charismatic worship may give that impression. No, the demands of love can be hard, as any parent knows, requiring difficult choices after anxious deliberation with the mind fully alert and the will steeled. We may fail in our difficult task, but when we admit our inability to love, we discover a new power of loving within us beyond anything we could expect. The rewards of love come only when we take the risk going out in trust towards others. Each time we do that we learn more of the mystery that is love, of the mystery that is God.

We need not be discouraged if we have to struggle with the idols that we have created or others have created for us: when we face the descent into the depths of our being we find more than we bargained for but that is where we meet the real God and experience the loving fathering and the creative mothering of God. Nor need we be discouraged when the language we use gives out on us: no image is satisfactory, no metaphor can encapsulate the mystery of God. Let the metaphors and analogies flow without worrying if they contadict each other, for truth is often found in paradox, in the tension between opposites. Let us dare to live in the tension, on the edge of our experience, reaching out to encounter the God who is the source of our being.

CHAPTER 6

DESCENDING INTO THE UNCONSCIOUS

Can I face the known and unknown
terrors of the way
and can I find it
when there is no map?

If I get there
where will I be?
Will it be the land of the enemy
or a land transformed
a land of milk and honey
after-forty years of wilderness
a land of summer sun
after a winter of darkness?
Will I want what I find?

I do not know that I am right to set out:
there is that within which says I must
I do not know where the path leads:
that within says I must follow
I cannot know
I can only trust

hard though that may be
History may tell with hindsight
but history has to be lived
forwards

The descent into the unconscious is dangerous. It is rather like trying to cross a trackless moor on a moonless night with the mist closing in. We may fall over the edge into a disused mine or sink into a bog without warning. We may encounter walls that have to be broken down to permit further progress on the journey. Some hills are so steep, some ravines so deep, that we have to turn aside or even retrace our steps until we can find another way forward. We may meet ghosts and spectres, dragons and demons. And all the time we shall be working in the dark or at best in the shadows, as this dream suggested to me:

On Christmas Eve railways close down
in time for Midnight Mass
or earlier if they can
It is already dark
as I leave London by tube
emerging from the tunnel
onto overground track
I know I have to change
I get out onto a dim platform
lit only by candles
and I wait for my connection
A train creeps in silently
at the other end of the platform
and is already gathering speed again
before I notice it
Was it my connection?
There is no one to ask
in this eerie station

and no food to be had
Will I get to my destination
before the trains stop running?
I am not far from London
and it's a long way to East Wales
Somehow I get on a steam train
which puffs its way slowly
along meandering tracks
stopping for me to change
from one empty train to another
at empty dark stations
I do not know whether I shall arrive
in time for Christmas or at all
I know I am going
to some place in mid-eastern Wales
but I don't know why
Mystery surrounds my destination
just as dark enshrouds the train
and closes in on me
in the unlit empty carriage
My unease moves into nervousness
and verges on panic
as I wake up

Do we need to undertake such a mysterious and risky journey? If we were well, perhaps not, but depression opens the doors of the unconscious, allowing us to edit the tapes on which the unconscious has recorded all the events of our life and the feelings surrounding them. Whether we like it or not, those feelings well up in our dreams by night and day and we find relief only by acknowledging them. And there are rewards. We may discover who or what in our unconscious is directing our way and so enable our greater self to take charge. We may achieve some integration of our personality or experience salvation, so that the warring factions within may make peace and live in greater harmony. We may hear the faint murmurings which communicate the wisdom of our greater self or the words of God, which tell us what is good for the whole self and not just the clamorous conscious ego. We may learn to love our whole self, warts and all. And what we learn on this dark journey will be a possession for ever.

The wisdom from the depths holds out hope
the hope that I shall be made whole
that I shall be healed
from the anguish of my tumultuous emotions
from my fear guilt anger and grief
That healing is wrought from and by love
the love which looks horror in the face
and still goes on loving

I doubt whether I would have had the courage to make the journey on my own. Without Jean's psychotherapeutic skills I might have baulked at the start as I had on previous occasions or turned back when the going got rough. Although she could not be much of a guide, because the journey was mine, the knowledge that she had survived a similar journey gave me the courage to persevere, as I struggled through the sewage of my unconscious:

Raw brown sewage spills
out of the manhole covers and the drains
flooding the garden
causing the lavatories to overflow downstairs
The smell penetrates the nostils of
those who suffer from septic tank drainage
and who have to deal with its ills
even reaching those on the top floor
whose lavatory and shower function still

compounding the confusion below

She complains
does the old woman down below
shouting up the stairs
You come down and sort this mess out
and stop running that water

He comes down
and paddles ineffectually in his wellingtons
prodding and pushing with the rods
to no avail
The sewage will not drain away
He shrugs and turns away
Leaving his boots by the door
he goes upstairs
to shower away the smelly sludge

Next day she's at it again
Will you come down from your ivory tower
and do something?

He does
The sewage slowly sinks
as he prods and pushes
leaving only a crust to dry in the sun
Success
but the crust reminds him
that his is no permanent solution
If the council won't connect the house to the mains
he must build a sewage works himself
A tank in which the raw sewage can settle
separating solids from liquids

Perhaps several tanks
so that there's plenty of capacity
A moving sprinkler
to distribute the liquid over the cinders
to purify it for return to the land

There isn't room in the garden
and the neighbours would complain
So there must be cooperation
with those in the same need
a communal sewage works
in land somewhat removed
so that the smell is not too bad
but not so far removed
that we forget the benefit
So he builds the works and lays the drains
The sewage moves slowly
as sewage does
towards and through the works
In the tanks the sludge slowly settles
while the liquid moves on
and out through the sprinklers
The sludge dries to form peat-like soil
to fertilise new growth on the common
which is watered by the purified liquid
And the old woman grumbles no more
for her room is filled with flowers
and she makes tea for the man from upstairs

What was the sewage? I came to see it as that part of my unconscious
which Jung called the shadow. It contained the mix of feelings that I
could not express at the time I felt them to the people who ought to have
been their recipients. Slowly I realised that I was not responsible for the

feelings that arose within me, but only for what I did with them. I had no need to feel guilty about owning them. To my own detriment I had unconsciously projected my emotions, letting other people carry them for me and feeling hurt when they were turned against me, or I had repressed them, letting them build up a head of steam until they burst out in inappropriate ways at an inconvenient time and caused my breakdown. I had so repressed many of my feelings that I could not even recognise what they were. I knew that I felt something but I could not put a name to it and I would have to ask Margaret what it was I was feeling. Because she is very perceptive she was often able to say, but that was not the same as saying what I felt myself. My repression also meant that I would often deny that I felt what she said I felt, so that I became touchy and self-righteous.

Gradually I learned to name what I was feeling in the present and what I had felt in the past. It was particularly important to name the feelings of the past, because I could then re-experience them and so defuse some of their power:

The healing for me comes
from feeling the emotions
of that abused child
from holding the child in love
from reassuring the child
that it is all right
to feel angry
hurt
rejected
sad
hateful
jealous
It is all right
because I am not responsible
for the feelings that arise within

but only for what I do with them
I try to acknowledge them
however hard my upbringing makes it
I try to let myself feel them
so that I can then decide
what I can best do with them
I know I do not need to hide them
from myself or even from others
for people may prefer
the real feeling me
to the medallion man
who seeks to pacify my own torment
and the chaos of emotion round about me
who takes responsibility
for everything and everyone around him

It is often said that repressed or unexpressed anger is at the root of depression. Certainly it was one of the roots of mine:

He struggled
late
to be born
As if knowing
he had to win their hearts
he smiled and gurgled
Helpless
his soul raged

Amid the ravings of the coven
he watched
helpless
as the witches' brew boiled over
causing the flames

fanned by the dragon's fiery breath
to rise ever higher
Helpless among the furies
he strove to hold up the cauldron
for fear of greater conflagration

The dance of the witches
led them in and out
of the fire's glow
As the leader went into shadow
he thought she had gone
through some fault of his own
He must strive even harder
to hold up the cauldron
lest he be punished
by something worse than fire
Helpless
he hung on
to the impossible

Year by year
the cauldron weighed heavier
The fiery brew scalded
and scarred his arms
The burgeoning flames
seared his body and soul
Because of the beginning
he could not relinquish
the impossible

Helpless
while rage consumed his being
he smiled

propitiated
reconciled
splitting his personality
light from dark
good from bad
love from rage
denying his wholeness
creating the angry
self-righteous
puritan
knowing so much
about God's righteousness
feeling so little
of God's love for himself

In the end
rage made him helpless
taking control
denying him life
threatening his death
yet helpless to control itself

How long
helpless rage
will you burn out of control?

The rage I felt had many sources: the circumstances of my birth and early childhood, my inability to cope with my overmighty father, my fear of my mother's cancer, my anxiety that the family was about to fall apart, the expectations that I had of others which were not fulfilled, the expectations that others had of me which I could not fulfil, and so on. Events within the family meant that rage could not safely be expressed and so I buried mine until psychotherapy made me aware that I was sitting on a time-bomb with the seconds ticking away, on a volcano about to erupt. What could I do?

Can I jettison it
throw it far away
hurl it into some forgotten corner
where it can do no harm?
Or will I merely project it
onto another
who does not deserve
the destructive gift?
Can I release its power
without creating more damage?
Or will I set off
another series of bombs
to burst on innocent heads?
Can I set it down
let it go
be free
from its weight and power?

The solution was none of these. It was a slow and piecemeal therapeutic process involving many steps. I strove to identify what made me angry in the present and the past and I learned how to express my anger in my drawing, painting or writing. It was rare that I could express it to those responsible, because some were dead and some could not take it, but I found relief in writing letters to those in power whose actions enraged me. I kept repeating to myself: it is all right to be angry. But I came to see that I needed to forgive those who had hurt me because harbouring anger and vengeful thoughts was letting them hurt me time and again, on the occasion of the original offence and on every occasion I re-experienced the emotions around it.

The healing comes too
from forgiveness
from going on forgiving the same hurts
each time circumstance brings them
to consciousness
going on forgiving
seventy times seven times
and maybe more

I practised ways of being more assertive, so that I could avoid being angry either with those who used what I later saw as moral blackmail or with myself when I was too weak to say no. I asked Margaret to pull me up when I used shoulds, oughts and musts, so that I took less responsibility for what was happening around me and was less angry if things went wrong. I tried to alter my assumption that life should be fair and to stop comparing myself with those better off than me. I looked for ways of being thankful for all the good things, especially those I so often took for granted. I resolved not to go on appeasing those who were angry with me and tried to respect their anger so that it frightened me less. To the question:

How long
helpless rage
will you burn out of control?

I could now reply:

Until you let go
relinquish the impossible
and allow the marriage
of light and dark
of good and bad
of love and rage

Then light will not blind
nor dark affright
Then good will not claim righteousness
nor bad be rejected
unforgiven
Then love will not be for others only
but embracing the self
will turn rage into energy
for the soul to recreate its wholeness

Rage is helpless no more

Of course there were and are many more negative emotions hidden within the shadow side of my personality, but anger will serve by way of example. There were and are other elements too: my parents and others whom I internalised and who unconsciously affected and affect how I behave. And what of the old women who called me down from the ivory tower or the little girl I recognised as the child in me at one stage? Perhaps they belong to chapter 7. But to be aware of the child within, to learn to respect his feelings and to love him was to allow him to grow past the blockages which impeded his development. It seemed important to communicate my love for him. Here is an imaginary conversation with him, which I wrote as two lines of a song by Patrick Brandon arose from the depths of my memory. I used them as the first two of the poem:

Come and sit down on my lap
and let me put my arms around you
Close the ears of your mind
to what they said
and listen to me
for I speak the truth
What they said is not true

It never was true
It never will be true
You are not bad

Listen and take it in
You are not bad
You may do things that are wrong
but you are not bad
and I love you whatever you do
You may have feelings of which you are ashamed
but you are not to blame
for the feelings that arise within you
but only for what you do with them
So you are not bad
and I love you whatever you feel
You need never hide what you have done
You need never hide what you think
You need never hide what you feel
because I love you whatever
If you are frightened by your thoughts and feelings
I will hold you
while we sort them out
so that you can come to terms with them
And remember I love you whatever they are
Listen and take it in
Let it wrap your heart around I love you
I love you small as you are
I love you
because I see the seeds of goodness in you
I love you
because I see the potential for growth in you
I love you
because you are you

Bathe in this love of mine
so that it seeps into every pore
that you know now and for ever
that you are rooted and grounded in love
that love is found in the depths of your being

CHAPTER 7

ENCOUNTERING THE FEMININE

A woman would use a different title, but I hope that what I say may be of use to women if they read masculine where I have put feminine. Several feminine images have already emerged from my unconscious: the little girl in whom I first recognised the child in me, the old woman who called me down into the sewage of my shadow self, and the witches who people some of my personal mythology. All of them may have contributed to the difficulty I have had in apprehending the feminine in God. But there was more. I have mentioned snakes before, but without drawing attention to their sexual significance:

Snakes inhabit my dreams
I wake terrified
Even if the dream disappears
from my consciousness
a nameless dread remains
I am struggling
to come to terms
with a female figure
mobile yet made of wood
with a snake
in a sinuous S-shape

carved on her-hip
crossing the grain
which follows the natural
naked line of her body
A snake is also carved on the hip
of a more shadowy male figure
I awake
knowing that I have to confront
the snake
now terrifyingly alive
which the cat is fighting off
for me
I am petrified

But how can I fight it
when I am awake
and it is gone
leaving its dread behind?

What is the female figure
of moving wood?
Is she the feminine in me
so real
so long denied?
She is beautiful
but for
and perhaps because of
the snake
Or is she the blond temptress
of another dream
with whom
despite the pleasure

I should not meddle?
What is the male figure
and why so shadowy?
Why is their beauty
enhanced and defiled
by the snake?

Am I back in the garden of Eden
with the snake
not as the tempter
but as original sin
part of the woman and the man
and part of me?

The trouble is
I don't want to acknowledge
that the snake is mine
for it terrifies me

I am grateful for the cat

There is another reason why it is hard to write about my sexuality: we derive our attitudes from our parents, a little from what they said, more from what they left unsaid, and most from how they behaved as male and female; and so whatever I say must in some way reflect upon my parents, though I make no judgements and give no details. One incident, which those involved would probably not remember, emerged from my memory during psychotherapy. Please do not try to imagine what it was: you are bound to be wrong because it was not what it seems. I was surprised by its appearance but the circumstances surrounding it have since been verified by another family member. The feelings around it were powerful:

No one tries to explain
that I have intruded
on something private
which is beautiful to the two of them
but which cannot be shared
No one reassures me
that it is their shock and shame
at being discovered
which unleashes the anger
Perhaps
they think
it is better to say nothing
to make light of it
so that I won't bring it up

Because I feel guilty
I say nothing

Silence allows the cancer of guilt
to grow around my nascent sexuality
twisting and perverting
so that bodily enjoyments seem wrong
yet powerfully attractive
so that delight in beautiful women
becomes a source of shame
so that I am shy to touch lest my touch
be too loaded with sexual meaning

I feel abused
and it is hard to forgive
myself
and those

Many sessions of psychotherapy and much drawing, painting and writing centred on the ramifications of this one incident. It affected how I felt about the female members of our family and caused me to deny those feelings to which the family gave feminine labels, even if in reality they are feelings common to both women and men. It rendered me less able to use the feminine both as a foil against which to develop my masculinity and as a pattern through which to interpret the women I would encounter. Although I buried the incident in my unconscious, there remained within me a determination that I should try to do things differently in a family of my own. Yet the complex and difficult feelings surrounding it worked from my unconscious like an agent provocateur intent upon sabotage. Paul's words became true of me: 'The good which I want to do, I fail to do; but what I do is the wrong that is against my will; and if what I do is against my will, clearly it is no longer I who am the agent, but sin that has its dwelling in me' (Romans 7.19-20). It seems that our sins as parents do descend to the third and fourth generation, or at least that our shadow side has the capacity to do harm until we face it and find ways to integrate it.

But I was hardly ready to face that, for I still had to face the changes that adolescence brought to my body and to my emotions. I could not talk to my parents and as was common in their generation they remained mostly silent on sexual and emotional matters:

A long embarrassed walk
father and son
together and far apart
means the birds and bees
are no fit subject for talk
No substitute for words unspoken
is found in healthy action

worthy of imitation
Strained relationships
lacking warmth and laughter
spontaneity and joy
do nothing to assuage
the anxiety and guilt
around the exploration
of male and female

Observing Janet's noisy but usually fruitless rebellions, I was outwardly cooperative and obliging (a better strategy for getting my own way) but I thought my own thoughts. I was fortunate to meet Margaret at an early age, and we parented each other through the turbulent times of adolescence. We might have done better to rebel openly, for we might then have established our emotional independence at an earlier and healthier stage. And parenting each other may not have been the best basis for courtship or marriage.

Coming as we both did from clerical families we could not fail to be aware of the Church's negative attitudes towards sexuality, some of which originate from the Old Testament. The Mosaic Law worries about the uncleanliness of menstruation (Leviticus 15.19-30) and birth (Leviticus 12), and places such emphasis on a bride's virginity (Deuteronomy 22.13-29) and on a wife's fidelity (Numbers 5.9-31) that a woman seems to be the property of her father or husband. Because it was believed that male sperm alone was the source of a foetus which the female womb only carried and nurtured, the Law was concerned to prevent the child of another man being foisted onto the father who had to provide for his unmarried daughters and share his inheritance among his sons. Old Testament morality was reinforced by stories which show how the power of sexual feelings can lead us astray, such as David and Bathsheba (2 Samuel 11-12) and Amnon and Tamar (2 Samuel 13). The impact on us was to override 'God saw all that he had made, and it was very good' (Genesis 1.31). If the Song of Songs was mentioned, no one treated it as a poetic celebration of the beauty and intensity of sexual love. How rarely is it used even today.

The New Testament seemed little better: it too has a low view of women. Eve is the occasion of Adam's sin (1 Timothy 2.8-15). Wives should be subject to their husbands as the Church is subject to Christ but husbands should love their wives as Christ loves the Church (Ephesians 5.21-33). Believing in the imminence of Christ's second coming, Paul recommends the single state (and Matthew 19.10-12 suggests that Jesus may have agreed), because the unmarried are 'concerned with the Lord's business' while the married are concerned with worldly affairs. Yet 'it is better to marry than burn with desire' and 'if you do marry, you do nothing wrong' (1 Corinthians 7). We were left with the impression that the desires of the body were essentially sinful, to be put to death by the spirit which brings new life to the body (eg Romans 8.9-13).

Although the early Church argued long and hard about what Paul meant, Augustine, with all the virtuosity of a smoker who has given up, gave what became the definitive interpretation. He argued that sexual desire was not natural but had entered the human race through Adam's sin, and so the Church came to uphold virginity as the ideal of holiness (witness the high regard given to celibate monks, nuns and priests) and to see marriage as second best. And when later on the Church moved to regulate marriage and to establish a wedding liturgy, its attitudes to sex were still begrudging: the Book of Common Prayer says that marriage 'is ordained for a remedy against sin and to avoid fornication; that such persons as have not the gift of continency might marry, and keep themselves undefiled members of Christ's body.' Sex, it seemed, was all right if it consummated the marriage sacrament and if it was within the marriage bond and concerned with procreation. Canon law, and the civil law which grew out of it, legitimised patriarchy and discrimination against women.

It was not surprising then that our long courtship created a conflict between our feelings and the beliefs inculcated by our clerical families:

There is light in her eyes
and bounce in her step
but steeped in puritanism
the Yes, it's lovely
conflicts with
the No, it's naughty
It is unhealthy for her and for him
the more so
the longer the years
before official approval is given

So we tend to think the ethic wrong which attempts to forbid sexual activity for the ever-increasing time which elapses between the earlier onset of sexual maturity and the later establishment of economic independence that makes marriage possible. Yet we take seriously the psychological truth which the Bible expounds and to which Jesus added his authority that sexual intercourse does create a pair bond: 'the two shall be one flesh' (Genesis 2.24, Mark 10.2-12). We are conscious too of the dangers of sex without love and commitment, even though modern methods of birth control make it unnecessary, in theory at least, to have the degree of commitment required to raise a child. Perhaps the Church should find ways of recognising the honesty of those young people who now openly live together before they get married. Might we return to the earlier practice of betrothal and dignify it with an appropriate liturgy, so that the sexual expression of committed love might receive a blessing? At least there would be honesty and young people might find their way into a Church that they now reject because they feel judged. A later wedding would signal a commitment to a marriage relationship of such quality and longevity as to permit the raising of children.

We felt committed to each other not only by the love we felt for each other but by the vows we made at our wedding: we believed that 'those whom God hath joined together let no man put asunder' (the Book of Common Prayer, based on the words of Jesus in Mark 10.9). It has been a source of strength to us, but we can see that just as monks and nuns may renounce their vows there may be circumstances in which a couple has no alternative but to renounce theirs. The Church might help such couples by devising a liturgy for repentance for a broken marriage, for the renunciation of marriage vows and for mourning the death of the marriage. The Church preaches that we all sin and that if we repent we may be forgiven and start again - unless we are married. The ideal may be the lifelong marriage, but we have to legislate for failure too. Part of that might be making it more difficult to become married: betrothal first? Some church people may be unhappy with this approach, but we should not read what Jesus said as creating a new law. His command, as argued in chapter 4, is that we should love, and love demands that we respond to each person in his or her circumstances. Morality is about people, not rules.

At the time I could not make sense of the wounds inflicted by my upbringing, but I began to see in my own experience how wrong was the Church's negativity towards the body and equally how wrong modern society was to idealise or falsify the body. Real bodies do not conform to the images on the screen, but yet the body is beautiful when it is the expression of a person engaged in the natural activities of a human being. I had the joy of watching Margaret's body develop in pregnancy and of sharing the birth of the child I had made with the woman I love: what could be more beautiful than Margaret's face covered in sweat and tears and joy as our baby came into the world? We should celebrate our beautiful bodies, and not fight shy of the Song of Songs. And we should celebrate the wonder and mystery which creates a new body and a new person from the fusion of two tiny cells in an act of love.

Our birth shares the mystery of creation

In part we understand
the mechanisms of nature
but not the purpose
But to the mother giving birth
and to the father watching
the natural process is transfigured
by their joy at the gift of a child
It is a miracle
a mysterious but commonplace miracle
when love gives birth to love
and eros gives rise to agape
We are made by love for love
and our life is a gift
to be treasured and enjoyed

Despite my wounded sexuality I began to see how the fullest communication between two people might lie in a sexual relationship. At its best sex represents the communication of two people through the medium of the body in a process which is aesthetic in one sense, mechanical in another, and yet transcends both. At its worst sex represents the exploitation of another's body, using it as an object, forgetting that a body contains a person and that people live on love and care. What counts is the love for the other person: if the aim is to communicate deep feelings of love, then the body may fulfil and be fulfilled; if the aim is to satisfy feelings of lust, then the body of the other will sense the exploitation and the relationship will suffer. So loving sex requires, like any effective form of communication, that we are honest, but it is difficult to be honest with the whole of our being when some of it lies hidden even from ourselves:

The negative within
lies concealed

until I feel threatened
and then
treacherously
sinuously
strangles me
and my beloved
The negative strikes at the roots
of my wounded sexuality
and coldly
irrationally
terrifies
and paralyses warm emotion
so that often I shrink
from contact
that may unleash the power
of the snake

Yet the Chinese say
the snake is born
under the sign of wisdom

What is that wisdom? It is learning to trust the best friend and love of my life, my soul mate on life's journey, to trust her love of me. I found this act of faith difficult, for in my shadow lurked the witches, untrustworthy and uncontolled women. Yet I did come to trust Margaret:

Love is the root of your being
love for yourself and love for others
It is not love of self
in the narrower sense
but love which accepts you
as you are

and sees what you may
with love
become
a woman for others
strong
as the yew is strong
not brittle like the oak
tender
as a mother is tender
with her babe in arms
not soft like an indulgent father
wise
as an old woman is wise
who has measured the seasons
and experienced life's sorrows
not clever like the man
who knows all the theory
loving
in the only sense that matters
with the interests of the other
at the centre of your concern

If I could trust her, I could be honest about the things I barely knew myself that psychotherapy was bringing to light. I could reveal the secrets of my true being. I started with some reluctance, as this attempt to make sense of a dream shows:

I don't want you to know
about my lumber room
It contains much baggage
people from the past
and the feelings they aroused

feelings which I daren't acknowledge
for fear of what they may do
to our marriage
Yet I know that feeling
unacknowledged
is still there
worming its way
into our relationship
wreaking havoc
that we do not expect
And I know
that you have a lumber room too
filled with the same sort of baggage

Yet still I fight to keep
my secret room
frustrating as best I can
your efforts to find it

I know some of what is there
I have unpacked some of the cases
burned the rubbish with glee
and kept what makes
a fitting memorial
to those people from the past
With some of the demons
left by those people
I have fought bitter battles
I have killed
two of the ghosts from the past
in furious fighting
but I have not come away

unscathed
I carry the wounds of battle
and fear you will find the scars
ugly or repulsive
So I hide myself in the lumber room
for many years
I'd like to sweep the room clean
so that you could enter
into light and warmth
but its corners are still dark and dank
and the light casts shadows
as it always will
If I invite you in
will you take the risk?
Can you accept the dark
and the light
for there is some light now?
Will you like the chiaroscuro
the patterning of light and dark
in the lumber room of my heart?
Can you love the bad and good
the actual imperfection
and the potential splendour
which somehow never comes?
Can you bear the dark secrets of my soul
and the energy released when they are told?

I'd like my shadows and yours
to grow together
in the light of our love
so that we do not play
the alternate game

me up
you down
and vice versa
I'd like us to relate
as adults and children
and not as the internalised parents
who judge us and others
from the lumber rooms of our minds
who interfere with our fun
and our freedom
as if to be free
and to enjoy full-blooded fun
was a sin

This life is not a rehearsal
for the next
We cannot earn a place in heaven
and we need have no fear of hell
This here
this now
is all we have
It is ours to enjoy
Why should demons and ghosts spoil it?
Let's kill them off

The incident which had so upset me when I was six and which had been buried for so long could now be put in a different light. In another poem the adult me spoke forcefully to the six year old within:

You don't need to feel guilty
about your anger
or about anything else

The primary responsibility was theirs
not yours
They were the adults
whose responsibility was to protect you
They failed
and felt guilty in the failing
and left you to carry the guilt
The guilt was theirs is theirs
You are not to blame
for a situation of their making
Refuse to accept the blame
Give it back to them
Even if they can no longer hear
say
This guilt is yours
Carry it yourself
or seek forgiveness on your own account
I will no longer carry it for you

Perhaps too you now can see
that you need not accept
their evaluation of you
or of your maleness and her femaleness
You need no longer accept
their words and deeds
which make sex furtive and dirty
You need no longer see
as through their eyes
the female as a temptress
designing to snare you
into repulsive unnatural activity
and the male's defence

as fight or flight.
You can look for yourself
and see
as if for the first time
that male and female are created
in the image of God
to love
and to create
through the union of body and soul
both the progeny of love
and the loving trustworthiness
to nurture that progeny
You can learn
to trust yourself
your feelings
and their expression
through the medium of body and mind

It was and is hard to grapple with the ghosts and demons that inhabit the shadow in my unconscious. They may never go away completely but I reduce their hold over me by refusing to believe their lies. Because they are cunning and dress up their lies as truth in their attempt to poison my relationship with Margaret, I have to be on my guard and remind myself of the wisdom learned in the darkness: I encounter the real feminine in Margaret and not in the phantoms of the past. We have the rest of our lives to enjoy that encounter, secure that I really know:

That I am fully and truly married to Margaret
That in marrying her I chose life
and have found true and abiding love
however difficult it is to live the life
and to accept the love

that cherishes her beloved for his own sake
That she is worthy of more love than I can give
though I hope to learn
how to give more of my real self
and less of the self I thought I ought to give
Pray God she likes it!

CHAPTER 8

DRAWING BACK FROM OBLIVION

Suicide is the worst violence
that you can perpetrate
on those you love
It is the ultimate rejection
worse than death
our death

I wrote these words some months after I had, finally I hope, conquered the impulse to kill myself. I use the word impulse, because I sometimes felt an almost physical compulsion to turn the car into a tree, so that I had to struggle to keep the car on the road or to stop until I regained control of myself. At other times I had the sensation of a noose around my neck which seemed to urge me to hang myself. I had no fixed intention to end my life - indeed I feared both the process of dying and what death might bring. But a 'brainstorm' - when faulty connections between the nerves of my brain made their messages go haywire and caused me to become intolerably agitated - might push me over the edge. I might indeed take my own life while 'the balance of my mind was disturbed.' If you have suicidal thoughts or feelings, please take them seriously and get help at once: a doctor is on call day and night and the Samaritans are always there for those who are desperate and suicidal (the number of your local branch is under Samaritans in the phone book).

Margaret, Roger, Jean and Bill took my suicidal feelings seriously and accepted what I was struggling to say with compassion and without judgement. Bill kept explaining that it was the chemistry of my depressed brain that was the origin of my suicidal thinking and he made the offer of a hospital bed as a safe haven if I needed it.

For a long time I felt that I was in a trap from which the only escape was death; that I was no good and people, even those I loved and who some part of me knew loved me, would be better off without me; that life had nothing left to offer. These thoughts had little basis in truth or reality: I was jumping to negative conclusions, ignoring all the good and positive things, and allowing my emotions to run away with my rational thinking. Jean reminded me that there is a way out of every trap, even if we may have to give up something precious. I found a way out: I gave up my job. It was hard to do and it took me two years to come to terms with it, but it saved my life and new life is gradually emerging from the ruins of the old. Having escaped I was no longer angry at being trapped, and so part of the anger that was driving me towards suicide was removed. Eventually I realised that I had made most of the trap for myself.

Even so I still felt that I was bad and unworthy of love. I came to understand that these feelings of unworthiness originated in my perception that I had failed to fulfil my father's ambitions for me, perhaps because I had been too sensitive like my mother. So, as described in earlier chapters, much of my psychotherapy with Jean revolved around taking authority away from the father I had internalised and giving myself permission to be who at the depths of my being I really wanted to be.

A simpler process went hand in hand with the psychotherapy. Margaret, Roger, Jean and Bill reminded me that there is always something we can give, even in the depths of depression: a smile, a prayer, a thank you, a touch - small things which show people that they matter - and I tried each day to do some of these small things. Margaret made me list the helpful and creative things I had done that week, that month, that year, in my life. They all told me, in their different ways, that my value to others does not rest on what I have done but on who I am. I kept counting all the people who loved me from a child on: even when I restricted the list to those who loved me for myself with no thought of return, a few whose love I valued thought I was lovable. If they thought so, perhaps I could learn to love myself. With the help of many people I began to see that, despite all the pain, misery, cruelty and selfishness in the world, there is much beauty: the flowers grow, the birds sing and the sun shines. I tried to train my eyes to see them and gradually I became more open to the kindness and love which is there if we look for it.

But the suicidal feelings continued, with particular crises when a friend's daughter took her own life and when another friend attempted suicide. Giving up my job allowed me time and space to explore in psychotherapy many of the feelings that I had repressed when in 1971 my sister Janet had died from an overdose of a sleeping drug. At first I wrote about her death in these terms:

In stark black on white
Poisoned by Welldorm
How we fought to avoid
in black on white
Suicide
or
Took her own life
while the balance of her mind
was disturbed
What we achieved
in black on stark white
was ambiguous

Poisoned by Welldorm
without agent
or motive
We know what killed you
without the who
or the why

The attempt to avoid the probability that Janet took her own life denied us the opportunity to come to terms with what had happened and with our feelings about it. I did not connect the depression which overtook me in the early 1970s with Janet's death, and so I did not begin to unravel my feelings until 1990. Then I began to name the feelings. Guilt, tinged with anger, came first.

We killed you
all of us who framed humanity for you
whose job it was to nurture
and to love you
For reasons both good and bad
or simply inexplicable
we failed to make you feel loved
so that you could play
the poor hand nature had dealt you
to the best effect

Could we have done better
if we had struggled harder
to love you
when you did so much
to make yourself unlovable?
Those who preach the love of God
for the unlovable

find it hard to practise
All of us are hypocrites
And those who love by will alone
are not perceived as loving
by those they claim to love
But you seemed to reject love
for love made demands on you
as well as on us
and you would fly
to the next person
who would love you on your own terms
Was your death a final rejection?
Did you intend to end it thus
cocking a snook at all of us
because we would not
could not
play according to your rules?
That would be a poor motive
and we would be right
to be angry

We did not intend to kill you
We merely wished you would go away
and our wish was granted
for you read our minds so well
So we are angry at ourselves
for we know
that we are all guilty
and we are angry at you
for you did the deed
which exposes our guilt

Can you remember the bright days
when you laughed and sang
danced and drove us to distraction
with your violin
when you felt generous
giving of yourself?
Can you think yourself
back to that mood
and forgive?
I shall try to forgive myself
but it is hard
when I remember
the dim sadness of the room
and the few things you left behind
A book of childish poems
and two violins
one broken
the other missing a string

Strong stuff! Perhaps too strong, taking more responsibility than was properly mine. Each of us must be responsible for our own actions, Janet no less than the rest of the family. But her death went on haunting me as I struggled with suicidal feelings of my own. It felt as if I were carrying the guilt of the family:

The noose around my neck
is not of my devising
I have no death wish
no wish to hang myself
It is others who wish
to choke the life-breath from me
lest I give voice to what I know deep down

even though I don't yet know what it is
It is better for one to die for the family
than for the family to die of shame

It is a thick sandy-brown hempen rope
twisted
and coiled around my neck
knotted at the back
as a hangman's noose

It chokes
as asthma choked my infant sister
making her blue in the face
whooping and gasping for breath
bent double
in the attempt to get air
to her punished lungs
She chose to punish them
rather than face the realities of life
She used her asthma at will
turning it on
as a weapon against her parents
not realising
that soon she would not be able
to turn it off
She deprived herself thus
of many joys
for the joy of doing others down
and in the end she killed herself
as surely as if she had put the noose
around her own neck

And she left the noose to me
I did not know of it before
I did not know that I must carry it
for the family
I did not know
that I must carry their guilt

But the noose rubs and tightens
as I try to give voice
to what lies at the depths of my being
I cannot
I cannot shout
I cannot speak
I cannot even whisper
the shame

But I was not alone responsible
for the train of events which led
to her death
I was only a bit player
Others had greater responsibility
and yet want me to carry the guilt
I will carry their guilt no more
See
I am cutting the noose
I have bought a sharp knife
with a curved blade
so that I can slide it
safely
between my neck and the noose
I saw it back and forth
It hurts my neck

and seems to take for ever
but at last the noose is severed
Wriggling like snakes
the strands fall away
and I am free

The last line was optimistic! There were more layers of feeling to be brought to consciousness before I was free from suicidal thoughts. I went to a workshop on forgiveness led by Joy Croft and Dori Veness at Ditchingham. It was a turning point for me, for I recognised that I needed to find forgiveness for my part in the tragedy:

I understand what drove you to it
better than you perhaps think
for I have been to that brink
but have been pulled back
by skilled and loving hands
I am sorry
that there were no hands
to pull you back
I am sorry
desperately sorry
that I took love
which you needed to live
Because I did not know
that I was doing it
logic says I am responsible
but not culpable
though that does not alter
the feelings of guilt
Can you forgive me
and if you can

can you tell me
from beyond the grave?
Can the dead forgive the living?

I need your forgiveness
or the guilt
however unrealistic
will overwhelm me
whenever events echo your death

The more aware I become
of my responsibility
of my unwitting but damaging collusion
in the sickness of our family
the more I have to confess
and the more I need forgiveness

Feeling the emotions which surrounded Janet's death and recognising my need for forgiveness seemed to remove some of the pressure to take my own life. But bigger breakthrough on that day at Ditchingham was the realisation that in the complex of my feelings around her suicide anger was dominant and that the best way to purge my anger was forgiveness.

Grief lost in the aftermath of death
and fury hidden by the relief
that you suffered no more
added fuel to the raging fire
created by the twisted history
of this sick family of ours
The fire lay buried
until its smoke issued

in the dark clouds of depression
Now that I can see the fire
I still fear its heat
and you added so much too it.
Perhaps however you had died
I would need to forgive you
but the hurt is greater
because you chose
how and when to die
without telling us
Can I forgive you
and if I can
can you hear me
from beyond the grave?
Do you need to repent
or to accept my forgiveness
before my forgiveness is real
and our relationship restored?
Can the living forgive the dead?

I have not forgiven you
I learned it this week
when ambushed once more
by grief and rage
I must forgive you
or be forever hostage
to the emotions frozen
by the shock of your death
When I understood
what you had done and why
I thought I had forgiven you
The more a man knows

the more he forgives
but knowledge is of the head
and forgiveness comes from the heart
I have not forgiven you
from my heart

I must picture you
saying
I am sorry
Please forgive me
and me replying
I forgive you
I absolve you
I must picture me
saying
I am sorry
Please forgive me
and you replying
I forgive you
I absolve you
We might even begin
to love each other

I extended this picturing to all involved in the tragedy. I had to repeat the process many times (and still do): I suspect that, when Jesus said that we should forgive our brother seventy times seven times (Matthew 18.21-22), he did not mean for that number of offences but for the same offence. The reality is that we forgive bit by bit as we discover that the offence still has the power to hurt. Yet gradually the picturing altered the way I felt and I concluded that it is a valid form of prayer:

My confession
often to be repeated

is to the God
at the heart of my being
and absolution comes
often repeated
if I listen
to the still small voice

I still had much mourning to do, but the emotions frozen at the time of Janet's death were thawing out and another death taught me how to mourn (see chapter 9). For the moment I was able to write:

I shall be glad to let you die
mourned as you should be
and forgiven
I shall be glad of another death
the death of grief and rage and guilt
so that I may rise to new life
with your forgiveness
and theirs and mine
and God's

I think that it was the weight of undifferentiated emotion that pushed me towards suicide. I feel less vulnerable to suicidal impulses now, partly because I have escaped from the trap that I had allowed my job to become, but mostly because I have slowly learned to name the separate strands of feeling and to deal with them individually. There came a point, after three years of psychotherapy, when I knew:

That I do not wish to kill myself
for that would be to collude
with the self-destructive curse
that the witches have cast upon my family

perhaps for generations
That I can override the curse
and deny power to the witches

CHAPTER 9

LEARNING HOW TO MOURN

The previous chapter makes it clear that I repressed my grief for Janet for many years. Superficially I felt relieved that she suffered no more and I was busy holding my distraught parents together: for complicated reasons my role in the family was to heal wounds and theirs were deep and intractable. Buried feelings fester and erupt later in inappropriate ways and at inconvenient times. A friend's funeral left me seething with anger:

I went to give thanks
in the sun-filled church
with the birds singing
I went to say
how much you meant to me
how sadly I miss you
how long you will live
in the love of my heart
I came away angry

Angry
at the insensitivity of certainty claimed

where there can only be faith
at the claim to know what is true
for me and for everyone
at the use of the Bible
as if this all-too-human record
has a magical authority
beyond the truth which speaks to my heart
as if it is the whole truth of God
the Word of God
in place of Jesus

Angry
at the limits placed upon the love of God
at the exclusion of all
who confess not Christ crucified
from the kingdom of God's love
at the failure to share that love with all
whatever the creed or lack of it

Angry
angry most of all
at the refusal to let you die
at the assurance of resurrection
reserved for those who love the Lord
giving false hope to some
bringing insecurity and even guilt
to many many more
at the inability to let you live
in the love of all our hearts
enabling us to find new life
in and through your dying

Alas for you

scribes and pharisees
hypocrites

Jenny, I am sorry
that anger got in the way
that emotions from the past
disturbed my worship
in the sun-filled church
with the birds singing

This funeral was in an Anglican church and the service assumed that for the faithful death marks a new beginning, but what of those who die holding no such belief? To use such a service for them encourages hypocrisy and to offer no service is unloving. Could not the Church offer an alternative which mediates the love of God to the relatives and friends of non-Christians without expecting them to endorse Christian belief? But more seriously the focus was on the hope of life eternal for the deceased with only brief acknowledgement of the needs of the mourners. Surely the service should more clearly affirm those who mourn, and perhaps the Church might offer other services to help people through the lengthy process of mourning. These are real shortcomings, but my anger was out of all proportion and, as we have seen, much of it belonged to the child in me and was directed at the father I had internalised. That father was in his forties, not the seventy-nine year-old that we had buried. How after all these years (he died in 1981) could I mourn this father of mine?

While I was struggling with these problems, we became involved with Daniel. He came to us for three days a week from about the age of two and for the last nine months of his life he lived with us because his mother was ill. From the start we knew that cystic fibrosis would cut his life short, but not how short. As part of our vetting as foster carers we were asked to write about a day in his life, to give the fostering panel some idea of what he was like and what his needs were. By this stage he had been living with us under respite care for some weeks, and he was three years and nine months old. This is what I wrote, with Margaret's approval and editing:

Seven-thirty: we are a bit late, for Daniel, disturbed by his dreams and his coughing, has woken us five times in the night. We need to be away by 9.20. Physiotherapy takes a good half hour, to the strains of Peter and the Wolf, which Danny enjoys while he follows the story in the library book. 'Is it library day today?' he asks, as he does every day. 'Yes, we can go this afternoon, for today is Tuesday. Monday play school, Tuesday library, Wednesday play school, Thursday Dr Beach, Friday play school and library, Saturday a day for an outing (his idea), Sunday church (he is fascinated by church architecture, stained glass and ornaments)' - that's how the week goes in theory, but he's only managed play school three times in a week once since he's been with us. The nebuliser takes ten minutes. And then breakfast: 'Oranges, please' - he is very polite. Margaret gives him one of his 'special drinks' while she opens the mandarins and prepares his many medicines. He drinks unwillingly after firm reminders, but he must drink, especially now that he may have jaundice. He has two spoonfuls of oranges and as usual he is sick, bringing up all the drink and lots of phlegm and mucus swallowed during the night (he has learned to spit it out when he's awake). So it's out with the bowl and disinfectant, and Margaret clears up - she's less squeamish than I am! Then we start all over again: he manages half a mug of tea fortified with 'Dr Beach's magic growing powder' and most of a yoghurt, and we get away at 9.25.

On Tuesday mornings we help with Riding for Disabled. Margaret teaches riders with severe learning difficulties who enjoy and benefit from their riding. Instead of helping as normal, I take Danny to Sheringham. I wrap him up well in the pushchair and we go to look at the steam engines. 'That is like Thomas. Those are Gordon's carriages. Those look like Annie and Clarabel,' and so he chats on. We do some shopping and suddenly he says he'd like a choc ice: he eats it with no fuss and no mess. We are back in time to see the end of the last ride.

More physio, more nebuliser - Margaret is in charge and, although she really enjoys it, she is aware of the effort it entails. Another yoghurt is all we can persuade Danny to eat for lunch. After his medicine, he sleeps while we talk to Sylvia about the arrangements for us to become temporary foster carers for Danny. Sylvia goes about 3.30, and then we're off to the library. He goes through all the Thomas books: 'I've read that...and that...and that' but finally he finds one he hasn't read. He then spends ages looking for Postman Pat: no joy, but we find five other books. He'll know them well by Friday. On the way back we visit Danny's Mum and he sits on her lap while she tells us that the hospital still has not told her what is wrong with her. Margaret says to Danny 'Poor old Mummy, it's such a shame her tummy still hurts, but she will get better and then you will be able to go and live at your house again.'

He opts for fish for tea. We pray that he won't bring it all up again, as he did yesterday. He holds it down and the medicine which follows, and he asks to play with the wooden train set. We set it up and snatch a few moments to get on with the chores. He normally likes to help, but there are many things that are beyond his strength or energy, and this is borne out today, for when we peep back at him we find him lying on the floor, holding the engine and almost asleep. I visit my mother in hospital while Margaret administers another round of physio and nebuliser; a quick bath and he's asleep by 6.30. We're in bed by 8.30, for we know our sleep will be broken, even if he has a good night.

Danny is very brave, accepting his fate with no complaint. Even when he is at his most distressed he is a ray of sunshine and a delight to be with.

On Good Friday, 29 March 1991, Danny was in hospital, a frequent necessity when medicine had to be given through a drip, but suddenly he took a turn for the worse. 'You realise,' said Dr Beach, 'that his illness is in an advanced state.' We knew his illness was terminal, but Danny had overcome so many setbacks that it came as a shock. On that Easter Sunday I protested:

Terminal means he will die
I know the medical causes
but they are not reason enough
why he should die before his time
I hammer on the doors of heaven
Why? Why?
but there is no answer
I scream at the unfairness of his fate
Life is not fair
but this is out of all proportion
I rail at the pointless suffering
I want to know
to understand
for it might then be easier to bear

Terminal means he will die
and I can do nothing to prevent it
No one can conquer death
except by accepting it
In time I may accept that I must die
and in the end he may welcome death
but I can't accept his death

though I know now that it will happen
Though I know
that life is best measured in quality
not quantity
I doubt whether there is anything beyond
to put right the injustice
So I rage still
and am sad
for I can't find Easter
in the midst of Good Friday

Naturally we all struggled with the mystery of suffering, and I found some comfort in the thinking which I outline in chapter 13. Two weeks before Danny's death I read Victor Hugo's poem *A Villequier*, in which he struggled to come to terms with the drowning of his sixteen year old daughter. I could not accept his argument:

You may be right
that the wheel of creation
cannot turn without crushing someone
Seas ebb and flow while eyes cry
Flowers bloom while children die
It happens
but do not say it is the will of God
Do not say it is the will of God
that your child has died

And yet many of us have a primitive sense that God is in charge and we are angry that God has let this happen to us. It is all right, it is healthy to be angry, but we are so often taught to restrain our anger, to bottle it up. It is far better to let it out, as I tried to explain in a poem which I wrote for Danny's mother:

Do rage
scream spit shout
howl and hurl abuse
God does not mind
if you curse him
He is in it with you
He is on his cross
on Good Friday

For all of us who loved Danny and were with him in the last two months of his life, it was indeed a long Good Friday. He needed more and more oxygen as there was less and less of his lungs through which he could breath and gradually he became weaker and weaker. Our anger was muddled up with so many other emotions. Had we done enough for him? How could we face the loss? How could we cope with a lingering death? And many more feelings were entwined in the muddle of our emotions as we waited for the inevitable:

Out of a lowering sky
a grey mist descends
befogging the senses
Emotions spin
around the dying of the young child
and I can see no way through the turmoil

The dying is hard
for him and for us
Would it be easier if he died tonight?
The lingering tears the heart strings
It hurts to see him suffer
It hurts to balance his needs
against those we have
we who will survive him

It hurts to live with the trauma of his dying
It would be easier if he were dead
We would know he was safe
from suffocation from within and without
from the premature grief
which makes him an object
for the emotions of others
rather than a person
to be loved through his dying

My experience of Janet's death made it hard for me, although my distress was nothing like the anguish of Danny's mother:

The dying is hard for me
for it echoes long-buried traumas
of pain anguish and death
It is hard to face death
when all I have known of death
is unloving and unlovely
It is hard to be loving
in the midst of echoes and ghosts

But still we struggled on at the edge of our capacity to cope and we got so used to coping that the end was a shock. And yet the shock seemed to unlock the other griefs of my life, allowing me to recognise, as if for the first time, how real were the losses I felt, and enabling me to mourn.

Even though I knew it would happen
and for his sake I wanted it to happen
it was still a shock
when he died
It was a numbing shock

and my senses are dulled
Sometimes I feel unutterably tired
as if depression had returned
in all its malevolence
At other times I dissolve into tears
at the slightest cause
He does not fill my thoughts
but my mind is abstracted
I cannot concentrate or remember
and I am overwhelmed by sadness
Yet he was not even mine
Has he unlocked hidden griefs
buried deep within
which now well up to engulf me?

Do I mourn for a sister
for whom I welcomed death
as a merciful escape from problems
neither she nor we could resolve?
How can I mourn her
who had her fair chance
and could or would not take it
when he had so little chance
and made so much more of what he had?
But perhaps I mourn the sister I never had
the might-have-been sister
who would give more joy than pain
whose mess I would not be left to clear up

Do I mourn for another foster son
whose going was as traumatic as dying
except that he lived
and we had to live with the guilt of failure

without the ritual of grieving his death?
Perhaps I mourn the son I never had
the might-have-been son
who would create more love than strife
whose mess I would not be left to clear up

Do I mourn for my father
who faced death and accepted it?
Do I mourn the strength of his intellect
and the power of his words?
Perhaps I mourn the father I never had
the might-have-been father
who would be more present than absent
whose legacy of frustrated grandiosity
I would not be left to clear up

Do I mourn the loss of my career
now that I begin to feel that I may work again?
Do I mourn the passing of my years
aware that I can no longer redeem the time
but must find wholeness with what I have got?
Perhaps I mourn all these and more
and perhaps I will rejoice
that I have had some chance to make amends
for the bad examples I have followed

But it is hard when my heart aches so

The answer to all of those questions is yes. I am aware now of these many griefs and a good few more. At times grief overwhelms me, I find myself crying and needing to work out what it is this time that I am mourning. I still find tears in my eyes for Danny, especially when I return to the moors where we said our last goodbyes to him:

The merlin circled overhead
and the peewits' cry rose above
the whistling wind and driving rain
We climbed
from the valley of the rooks
to the summit of the moor
Under a fragment of blue sky
we laid a cross of wood
against the cairn
finding stones to anchor it
But you we let fly free
with the merlin
as we wept
in each other's arms

Yet I am learning to recognise and to separate the sources of the different feelings of grief and to allow myself to mourn. And giving myself permission to mourn has removed some of the leaden weight of depression. In particular I have learned to mourn the loss of my might-have-been childhood:

Only the ability to mourn
what I lost in my childhood
can heal me
I can only know what I lost
by experiencing once more
the real feelings of childhood
and they are buried
deep inside the idealised
conforming
false self
that is the me

I present to the world
and to myself

In imagination I spoke to my mother in what now seem such sad words. As I wrote them I knew I could never saying anything like them to her, even though in her eighties she was stronger psychologically than she had ever been.

It was not me you loved
but what I pretended to be
because I knew
what you wanted me to be
not like the others
but smiling and conciliatory
not free
to express the real emotions
that swept the infant me
I knew I could not voice them
for fear of losing your love
and your love was not strong enough
to hold me while I experienced
what I really felt
I needed your love
so that I could grow
but you loved a me that wasn't me
a me that sought in others
mother love that could accept
my rage and hatred
and so prevent me from turning them
on myself
But how could you love
someone you did not know?
The cleverness of my speech

veiled my true feelings
It veils them still
The true me is hidden and lost

Facing the feelings of the sad child in me was an important part of the mourning. Over months I grappled with my fear, rage, guilt, and finally, loath though I was to admit it, hatred. Naming these normal feelings, I was able to experience them. With trepidation and reluctance I found ways to express what should have been expressed many years before. But there still seemed to be a blockage.

The feeling of desolation is real
because I am not alone
with a familiar friendly me
but alone
at best with a sense of emptiness
and at worst with a terrifying stranger
How can I offer myself
in love and friendship
if I don't know whom I am offering?
There is indeed a time to weep
and a time to mourn
The time is now
and perhaps the time is long
I may never be filled with gaiety
and I may never be free from pain
but I look forward to renewed vitality
to being alive
as the me I really am

Is that too much to hope?

It was many more months before I came to recognise that God loves me whatever and so I can love the self that I really am, but that story belongs to chapter 12. First I had to confront my own mortality, for the death of those we love reminds us that we must die one day.

CHAPTER 10

FACING DEATH

Events in my life have brought me close to my own death: I have wrestled with the powerful urge to kill myself and I have faced the deaths of others, some close to me and some in tragic circumstances. I know now that I do not want to die before my time and that there is too little time left to do everything that I think worthwhile and that I enjoy. I was convinced of this by a workshop entitled 'Living your Dying' led by Brian Thorne. In the workshop we explored our ideas of death and through a meditation we were helped to experience our own death. And afterwards I wrote:

I shall not want my death
when it comes
I may deny the reality
beg and plead and bargain
be fearful and cowardly
but I shall not want it
because I have so much to live for

For years my denial of my feelings about Janet's death prevented me from facing my fears about my own death. Anyone's death touched on those feelings and fears and so I colluded with society's efforts to sanitise death and convinced myself that I should not intrude on anyone's grief. What a fine excuse for my own cowardice and what a lack of love, for we who grieve are often lonely and want someone to listen so that we can sort what we feel. I could not escape from Danny's death and learned that I must face my fear. I began by reading *On Death and Dying* by Elizabeth Kubler-Ross and this is what I then wrote for Margaret:

I have not been able to accept
in the depths of my unconscious
that I am going to die
So I have colluded
with society's attempts to deny
the reality of death
But I know now
that I shall die
and for me an after-life is no more
than a religious way of denying
the reality of death
So I shall become extinct
What I have done or said
may have an impact for a while
for good or for ill
But the thinking and feeling me
will think and feel no more
and that is the reality of death

Many Christians will disagree, proclaiming everlasting life in the presence of God for those who die in faith. Even if we can put on one side the difficulties raised by those who die without faith (surely a loving God cannot abandon them), the traditional picture of life after death seems to deny the reality of death and to deprive us of the capacity to mourn our loss. But, many Christians say, the Bible and the Church assure us of everlasting or eternal life and that should be evidence enough. Not really, for the language used is not scientific or objective but analogical and metaphorical. None of us, not even the writers of the Bible, have direct evidence about life after death, and so at best we can only be agnostic about it. We may feel so close to loved ones who have died and they may have been so precious to us that we cannot conceive that death is final, and we hope to be reunited with them one day. Or we may believe in life after death because life makes little sense if goodness is not finally rewarded or if there is no compensation for the rotten deal some have in this life (how we cling to the notion that life ought to be fair!). Even as I wrestled with Danny's impending death, I could not bring myself to go further than this:

I fear the death
of this young child
It is the worse
for he has done nothing
to bring it upon himself
nor has he had a long full life
He is a part of me
and I know not where he goes
An after-life seems a false comfort
though I would not deny it
to those who can believe
The most I can believe
is that he will live in the hearts
of those that love him
but will that be enough
to face the finality of death?
As night falls
the grey mist deepens the darkness
the darkness of forboding
And all we can do

is to let the darkness come upon us
which shall be the darkness of God

But many Christians rest their case for life after death on the promises of Jesus and/or on the resurrection. Even if we can establish what Jesus actually said about life after death, there is little agreement on how we should interpret it. And I argue in chapter 11 that the only verdict we can return on the physical resurrection of Jesus is unproven. An interesting passage in Matthew (22.23-32) suggests that Jesus did not see life continuing after death much as before and believed that 'God is not God of the dead but of the living.' John (17.3) has Jesus saying 'This is eternal life: to know you the only true God and Jesus Christ whom you have sent.' This suggests that eternal life is life in tune with the ground of our being, in fellowship with God and in response to the claims of love upon us, life of a new quality, an eternal quality which is beyond time, for it does not come after time but is found deep within it. It is this quality of the timeless within time that T S Eliot explores in the *Four Quartets*, from which the last two lines of the poem above are taken.

Whatever view we take about life after death, we have to be careful that a belief in the rewards of a future life does not prevent us from living our life to the full, treating all life as precious and exerting every effort to further God's love and justice in this world. To the question, 'What must I do to win eternal life?' Jesus gave a very practical answer, 'Go, sell your possessions, and give to the poor' (eg Matthew 19.16-26).

So, although I may hope for life beyond death, my life may end in extinction, and that is almost inconceivable when all we know is our consciousness of life. My contemplation of what the end of consciousness might mean started from my fear of the process of dying. This is more of what I wrote for Margaret:

I fear my dying
certainly the pain

but more the lack
of dignity and humanity
which surrounds dying in hospital
I'd like to die
where I can be loved
through the process of dying
rather than be treated as a body
whose life is to be saved
or prolonged to the last second
whatever my spirit may say
I'd like to die at home
in my own time

At times you know well
I was too busy
picking up the pieces
of other people's grief
to feel or express my own
This unfelt unexpressed grief
I have felt as fear
and I have shrunk
tongue-tied
from the dying of others
Even now that I have done some mourning
I still shrink inside
when I know I should go out
in love
to those who are dying
and to those who watch
in grief

I do not want to shrink

from my own dying
If I can know when I am dying
I want to know
I want no kind conspiracy of fear
which presumes to know
better than I
what is good for me
I shall know anyway
So tell me the truth
as you have always done
Tell me gently and persistently
even if I attempt to deny it
so that I can try to conquer my fear
and experience some of the quality
of eternal life
in the shortness of time
that may remain

And if I am angry
I ask for patience
However much I displace my anger
finding fault with this or that
it is not with you
that I shall be angry
but with my situation
when I see it for what it is
If I am angry
that my life is to be interrupted
with so much unfinished
help me to express my anger
in safe and healthy ways
and to rid myself

of the envy I may feel
for all who enjoy the fullness of life
before it destroys my humanity

And if like the criminal
who turns Queen's Evidence
I try to bargain for a lighter sentence
ask what I feel guilty about
or what I feel rather than think
about God heaven and hell
for real healing
is of the mind and spirit
which is possible
up to the last moment

And if I am depressed
as I may well be
help me to solve the practical problems
over which I have lost control
and if I despair
hold out to me the hope of healing
though not of cure
the hope of the final acceptance
that will banish fear
But let me prepare for dying
by mourning the loss
of all whom I love
and all that I hold dear
Let me be sad
Sit with me in silence
or hold my hand
and murmur sweet nothings

I shall be sad
to let go of you
and don't be hurt if I begin
that letting go before I die
It will not mean I love you less
Instead be sad with me
for I shall need you to let me go
before I die

Imagining what at first seemed unimaginable enabled me to say to Margaret, lest the circumstances of my death should prevent me from telling her at the time, how much I love her and how grateful I am to her for her love of me:

I am grateful beyond words
for all you have meant to me
We have enjoyed a precious love
and a rare and instinctive trust
born out of empathy and intuition
and refined by suffering
I shall love you always
through and beyond the grave
Allow yourself to mourn
but don't allow your conditioning
to exaggerate your guilt feelings
You have been
and you are
the best wife in the world

Facing our final extinction may enable us to accept that life is a series of smaller deaths: youth, health, employment, friendships, love, and much more may die on us. How we handle death in life determines whether or not there will be life after death.

In the midst of life is death
After death in this here and now
there can be resurrection
to a new and different life

I have already referred to the death of my career (see chapters 1 & 9). It was only when I recognised it as a death and named the feelings around it that I was able to mourn and to rise again to new life:

I have another death to mourn
the early demise of my career
the laying down of my job
of power
position and status
I let it go unwillingly
with anger
that I no longer had the health and strength
with guilt
that I was taking the easy way out
with sorrow
that I must leave
what I loved and hated
what I knew and felt married to
with relief
that I need no longer struggle
with joy
at new found freedom
with anxiety for future security
with surprise
that there is life after education

As I write I am experiencing a kind of resurrection in my life, a real resurrection after a real death, with new shoots of growth emerging from the ashes of my former professional life. What I had to face was perhaps easier than the death of a major relationship: those involved in the death of a marriage or of a close love-relationship need greater support than we may realise. I experienced another kind of death in the role reversal required by the decline into old age and ill-health of my mother. The mother who parented me became the little old woman who needed my parenting. It was a gradual process, one which I sometimes resented and fought against, but not one which I thought to mourn, until illness forced my mother to move into a nursing home. Then I found myself plunged into deeper depression and for some time I could not work it out. I struggled with the muddle of emotions that contributed to the blackness of my mood. At first she hoped she would be home in a few weeks, but it was soon obvious she would have to remain in the nursing home for the rest of her life. How I struggled with it:

There you sit
crumpled
shrunken
and in pain
You are so hard of hearing
that communication is difficult
even if I knew what to say
Perhaps you do not notice
that I am tongue-tied

Part of me wants to say
how sad and sorry I am
that you must now depend upon others
when you struggled so long

to be independent
It was a noble fight
You won the psychological battle
(you did become your own person)
as you lost the physical war
But the war is lost
even though you will not come to terms
I shrink from telling you
that there is no alternative
to the nursing home

I feel guilty
because I cannot care for you
in our home
The doctors say
my health will not take it
but I know
that the difficult history
of our family
and of the relationship
between you and me
makes it impossible
I cannot tell you
frail and aged as you are
how it was for me
and how your actions now
create echoes of actions long ago
stir up emotions long-buried
in the mud of the unconscious
and make me as vulnerable now
as the child I once was
How sad it is

that I cannot tell you the truth
and never will

Fortunately my mother made the decision herself to stay in the nursing home and asked us to sell her flat. Clearing out the flat triggered many of the emotions around my childhood, many painful and some to be treasured, and I had to face the sad truth that I could never now tell her how I felt about my childhood. I could never put things right, perhaps through the sort of healthy row that teenagers have with their parents followed by the mutual forgiveness that restores a loving relationship. An opportunity had gone for ever. A part of my life had died, though my mother still lived. Early in my psychotherapy I had a dream and wrestled with its question:

Mother is dead
the dream said
She is alive
How can she be dead?

Now I knew the answer and hoped for a resurrection. What kind of new life could there be? The relationship could not be made new again, to become the might-have-been relationship that it never was. It could not be renegotiated, as maybe it should have been in my teens. She had not been well enough then and now she never would be. It seemed like a dead end, but it was not. There were things I could do. I could work out once more what it was that I really felt, so that I could mourn this death in the midst of life. I had thought that I had already done that, and it came as a shock to find still more to be acknowledged and worked through. I came to see that my anxiety and panic was that of the child in me when my mother was taken to hospital in life-threatening circumstances that were not explained to me. I knew from my own experience as a sick five year old that hospitals were not nice places:

The drive to the Victoria hospital
winds upwards through dark trees
to a grey pillared portico
The door opens onto a dim hallway
and we tread loudly and fearfully
across the marbled floor
The Xray machine is cold
its verdict incomprehensible
What is a shadow on the lung?
No one tells me
but I am banished to bed for a year
for an eternity of punishment
for a crime
I am not aware of committing
Yet my prison is a cause of envy
to others who would be the centre of attention
It is a large room
on the sunny side of the house
overlooking the Miners' Home
where lung-damaged miners take
the ozone-laden air of the North Shore
It is a solitary confinement
with meals at regular intervals
but with no visitors except Dr Baird
and I feel no love

Because I did not at first make these links, I could not name the anxiety I was feeling and so it felt like depression. Once I recognised it, I could comfort the child within:

I need no longer feel contempt
for my weakness and anxiety

for it is only a defence
against childhood feelings
Unacknowledged
they create the nameless dread
and the black moods of depression
which engulf me without warning
Despised and unwanted they may be
but they are real
they are mine
and I must not belittle them

I found too that I needed to forgive the hurt caused by hiding the truth from me. I began to imagine myself forgiving my parents in the same way as I forgave Janet (see chapter 8). I hoped that my mother would find the healing that love and forgiveness may bring. Even though there was no hope of a medical cure, she might rest in peace for the remainder of her life, untroubled by any fears and anxieties that I might bring into her sick room. And I tried to forgive my own collusion in the fear of illness with which she infected our family, but my own strength was not enough to forgive her or myself, to bring about the resurrection that would create new life in this relationship which had died.

Can God forgive the sins
of the fathers and mothers
sisters and brothers
unto the third and fourth generation?
God has so much to forgive
them and me
for I have colluded in their sin
and made of it my own
Can God forgive so much?
He could and should

if he is worthy of my belief

But it is awfully difficult
to believe

I concluded that I needed to seek God through Jesus and to ask forgiveness, but even as I reached this conclusion, I knew that my attitude to death had changed, as one of my pictures suggested. I developed the image as I punted on the Cam one summer afternoon:

The punt plashes through the water
The leaves fall early in the August heat
The hum and twitter of wildlife
become loud in the silence
and there is no need for words
Lingering eyes smile
as sun and shadow pattern the water
and feast
as birds and insects wheel and dive
over meadows of buttercups and bees

Punting lazily upstream
towards the source
the image is formed
before we reach the Old Vicarage

The pole is rough and wet
scattering droplets on cushions
damping sleeve and trouser-leg
but causing no discomfort
for the day is still warm
This day is a foretaste

of the journey to come
The river winds
both straight and true
Returning to the source
is what all must do
as night falls
and the way is lit
by the wisdom of the moon and stars

But the meadows are pleasant yet a while

CHAPTER 11

DISCOVERING JESUS

Jesus bids us shine with a pure clear light
like a little candle burning in the night.
In this world of darkness we must shine,
you in your small corner and I in mine.

As a small child I did not know who the Jesus of this children's hymn
was, but I had a vivid picture of a candle trying in vain to dispel the
bedroom dark of which I was very much afraid. Could this Jesus keep
the fragile flame alight or increase its power to conquer the dark? It did
not seem so then, but my childhood picture stays with me and the
question persists: who was or is Jesus?

Jesus asked his disciples much the same question (in Matthew 16.13-
23): 'Who do you say I am?' Peter declared his conviction that Jesus was
the Messiah. Accepting Peter's faith but leaving it unclear whether he
accepted the title or not, Jesus told the disciples to keep their belief
secret. Why? Perhaps because people had preconceived ideas about the
Messiah, expecting him to be a mighty leader who would deliver Israel
from the yoke of Rome or a heavenly king of glory. Jesus knew that he
could not fulfil such expectations and he told his disciples that his
mission would end in suffering, death and resurrection. When Peter

rebuked him for his vision of what was to come, he responded with 'Out of my sight, Satan.' As I became more depressed the Jesus I met in church and in much conventional writing seemed a cardboard cut-out figure whom the Jesus of the Bible would reject. How could I find a Jesus who became real to me, who spoke to the fullness of my heart and mind, who might save me from the darkness of depression? I felt I must empty my mind of preconceptions and come fresh to the evidence.

My first approach was historical. The New Testament evidence about Jesus is overlaid by twenty centuries of the Church's writing and preaching about Christ and even the Gospels were written as material for the preaching of the early Church, not as history. How could I find the Jesus of history? From non-Christian sources we know a lot about Palestine in the time of Jesus and the Gospels get most of the details right: that would not be so if they were forgeries. The Gospel accounts vary according to the perspectives and purposes of their authors, and if they did not, we should suspect collusion in a deception. So I could accept the Gospels as authentic sources, from which biographical details might be gleaned, without acknowledging everything within them as history. Sometimes it is argued that, if the miracle and resurrection stories in the Gospels are not true, then the whole story is invalidated, but that is the fallacy of the excluded middle. Historians do not dismiss Bede because he includes miracle stories but instead ask what function those stories serve in the *Ecclesiastical History*. I could do the same for the Gospels, reading them as myth or parable when that seemed warranted.

Few biographical details about Jesus emerged. The son of Mary and Joseph and brother of James, Joseph, Judas and Simon and of two or more sisters, Jesus lived in Nazareth and worked as a carpenter. Aramaic was his first language, but he spoke and read Hebrew. In his early thirties he was baptised by John and became an itinerant teacher and healer. After a ministry in Galilee he went to Jerusalem, where he was executed one Passover Friday, on the orders of the Roman procurator Pontius Pilate following trumped-up charges brought by the Jewish authorities.

The Gospels are imprecise about dates, but the best estimates seem to be around 6 BCE for his birth, perhaps 28 CE for his baptism, and 30 or 33 CE for his death.

The Gospels show a person of original mind, whose thinking is expressed in simple words rather than complex ideas (eg Matthew 5.21-24, 6.25-29, 7.1-5); in poetry, whose Aramaic and Hebrew forms are still partly visible after translation into Greek and then into English (eg Matthew 5.3-10); in parable, which uses everyday examples to make profound truth accessible to all; in dialogue and question rather than in direct statement, and often with an ironic turn of phrase. The parable of the good Samaritan (Luke 10.25-37) uses simple language and familiar figures to show how one of the despised Samaritan race could be more loving than the conventionally good priest and Levite - Jesus was surely aware of the irony and paradox in choosing a good Samaritan - and the parable arises from a dialogue with a lawyer who is left to draw his own conclusions.

I heard the most authentic voice of Jesus in those passages of Greek which bear the imprint of translation from the Aramaic, in the parables and in the pithy and often paradoxical sayings which Matthew collected together in the Sermon on the Mount (Matthew 5-7). I have pondered this teaching and some of it has come to life in me and for me. Perhaps, as is the way with parable and paradox, more will evoke a response in me as I continue to meditate upon it.

If Jesus is the word of God
God's self-expression
in human form
the way God seeks to communicate
to humanity
about the humanity of God
how does God speak
through Jesus?

In stories
that I can ponder
in my heart
rather than in doctrines
that I can analyse
in my mind
and so argue about
or oppose
Carrying a story
in my active memory
I may make it my own
not learning its moral
but accepting it
as a part of myself
coming to live it
as a true myth
altering the way I feel
at the depths of my being

In paradox
holding together two truths
apparently self-contradictory
so that I live
in the tension between the two
without accepting one
and denying the other
so that the tension becomes
the spring of creativity
within my greater self

Clearly people recognised the authority with which Jesus spoke (eg

Mark 2.23-27), and believed him when he forgave their sins (eg Luke 7.36-50). John indicates that Jesus attributed that authority to God (8.28-29, 14.24), but John may have made Jesus voice John's interpretation: as Greek has no inverted commas it is hard to decide where Jesus stops speaking and John starts commenting, and modern versions vary in their punctuation. Whatever, Jesus was not afraid to use his personal authority, as in his devastating denunciation of the scribes and pharisees (Matthew 23.1-33, Luke 11.37-54), or to exercise his powers of healing and exorcism. I found myself accepting the authority of what he taught, because it rang true with some deep chords in my being, and slowly his teaching cast light on the deep shadow of my depressed personality (see chapter 12).

I began to piece together the core of his teaching. Luke 4.16-30 tells how Jesus began his teaching in the synagogue in Nazareth by quoting Isaiah 61.1-2 to point to the year of God's Jubilee, the fiftieth year in which the Law ordained land should be returned to its original owners and be allowed to lie fallow, debts should be forgiven and Israelite slaves released (Leviticus 25.8-55). Jesus used the idea of the Jubilee to announce the Kingdom of God, where love and forgiveness are offered first to the poor in spirit and the poor in material things. He reinforced this message in the Beatitudes (Matthew 5.3-12, Luke 6.20-26). Jesus makes the offer to the poor because they know their need: some of Jesus' parables point out how easy it is for wealth (eg Luke 12.15-21, 16.19-31) or religious observance (eg Luke 18.9-14) to lock us into the way things are and stop us responding to the demands of love.

Mark has Jesus starting his ministry with 'The Kingdom of God is upon you. Repent and believe the gospel' (1.15). Repentance means changing direction away from the things which hold us back and towards finding our true selves, towards doing the will of God. The gospel, the good news, is that God loves us and accepts us as we are, whoever we are, and freely offers forgiveness, whatever we may have done (Luke 15.11-32). Despite his great sin, the prodigal son is forgiven because he knows that he needs forgiveness, but his older brother does not recognise his self-righteousness and so feels jealous that there is joy over his brother's repentance (see chapter 12). Jesus aimed several parables at the self-righteousness of the pharisees (eg Matthew 20.1-16): God loves us all equally and no one can claim a privileged relationship with him. All can enjoy a close relationship with God and know that we are loved and accepted. Once we feel loved we can love ourselves and others, and the parable of the sheep and the goats tests how honestly we accept and respond to God's love for us (Matthew 25.31-46).

Jesus also taught by healing, and his healing miracles are sometimes cited as proof of his divinity, but we need to be cautious. There have been other miracle-workers, and Jesus rejected miracles as a way of winning support (eg Matthew 4.5-7) and rebuked those who asked for miraculous signs (eg Mark 13.21-22, Luke 11.29-32). He preferred 'sign' to 'miracle,' seeing his works of healing as signs that God's love and forgiveness were at work (eg Matthew 9.2-8) or that faith was effective (eg Mark 5.21-43). Because we now understand something of how Jesus might heal seemingly incurable conditions without supposing that he or God interfered with the laws of nature, we may attribute some of his miracles to writing that wished to emphasise his extraordinary gifts. Two such might be the turning of water into wine at the wedding in Cana (John 2.1-11) and the feeding of the five thousand (eg Mark 6.30-44), though the latter may have the simpler explanation that willingness to share creates plenty for all. None of this devalues the healing miracles of Jesus, for God's love and forgiveness are not lessened nor the role of faith. And each healing testifies that disease is not God's punishment for sin and God has a special concern for the sick. We should rejoice in the miracles of Jesus and in the 'ordinary' miracles which love, forgiveness and faith bring into our lives.

I liked the way that Jesus stepped beyond the conventions of Judaism to offer love and respect to the poor, the sick, the outcast and the downtrodden. He was criticised for spending time with tax-gatherers and sinners (eg Mark 2.15-17). He challenged the patriarchal harshness of the Law so that the woman caught in adultery might repent (John 7.53-8.11). Perhaps his relationships with women were the most surprising. His disciples were astonished to find him talking to a women at the well of Sychar, for it was thought undesirable for a rabbi to converse with a woman (John 4.27). He accepted the touch of a woman rendered ritually unclean by twelve years of menstrual problems (eg Mark 5.25-34). And women were numbered among his companions (Luke 8.1-3) and close friends: he stayed with Martha and Mary at Bethany (Luke 10.38-42, John 11.1-12.8), while Mary Magdalene, whom Jesus evidently healed (Luke 8.2), features prominently in the stories of his death, burial and resurrection. We have much to learn from his refusal to accept the patriarchal norms of the society in which he lived.

I deliberately tried to keep the teaching of Jesus separate from the teaching of the Church about Jesus, but it was hard because the early Church's ideas of who he was moulded biblical accounts. We can see how those ideas grew: John's christology is more developed than that of the synoptic Gospels which are in turn more developed than the writings of Paul. Could I discover who Jesus himself really claimed to be? Could I find scholarship which was not conditioned by two thousand years of Christian theology? I turned to *Jesus the Jew* by the Jewish scholar Geza Vermes.

Vermes argues that the Jesus of the synoptic Gospels believed that he was a prophet in the line of Elijah (though Christianity has made little of it since); he accepted the title of lord as the Aramaic form of address to a teacher or miracle-worker (but not in the sense of 'the Lord' which referred to God); he was equivocal about the title of Messiah (many dismiss the only definite 'I am' in Mark 14.61-62 as the only direct claim in the synoptics for there are variant readings in the manuscripts which tally with Matthew 26.63-64 and Luke 22.67-71); he referred to himself about sixty times as 'the son of man,' usually as a circumlocution for 'I' (references to Daniel 7.13-14 which had acquired Messianic meaning by the first century CE may not be the actual words of Jesus); and, even if he accepted the title of 'son of God' from the lips of others, he and those around him probably understood it differently from the definitions of the creeds.

The Gospel of John has Jesus making many direct claims about himself. If he did make them himself, it is odd that none is included in the synoptic Gospels, and perhaps we should read them as John's theological understanding of the role and significance of Jesus for the early Church. In the accounts of Jesus' trial even John has Jesus refusing to confirm or deny that he is 'the King of the Jews' (18.33-40, cf Matthew 26.63-64, 27.11, Mark 14.61-62, 15.2, Luke 22.67-23.3). But there is much evidence in John and the synoptics that he saw himself as the Suffering Servant in the terms of Isaiah 40-55 and spoke of his role as a servant (eg Mark 10.42-45, John 13.1-17) and of his coming suffering (eg Matthew 16.21, John 10.14-18). Whenever John has Jesus saying 'I am', the passage frequently refers to the special relationship of the Son to the Father (6.30-58, 8.12-19, 10.1-18, 11.21-27, 14.1-14, 15.1-17), and John seems to claim an identity between Jesus and God.

Was this what I must understand when Jesus was called the son of God? Vermes argues for another interpretation: the Old Testament applied the title to angels or heavenly beings, to Israel or Israelites, and to the kings of Israel, and the Church has seen this divine royal sonship descending naturally to Jesus, the Messiah-King. The Jewish contemporaries of Jesus did use 'son of God' for the Messiah, but it was also an Aramaic form of address for a teacher or a miracle-worker, often commended by a heavenly voice, as Jesus was at his baptism (eg Mark 1.10-11) and at the transfiguration (eg Mark 9.2-8). It may be in this sense that those 'possessed by devils' recognised Jesus as 'son of God' (eg Matthew 8.28-29). Whatever the origins of the title, it is not necessary to infer from the synoptic Gospels that Jesus and God shared the same nature. The birth stories and the adoption and enlargement of several contemporary titles may be attempts by the Gospel writers to indicate the specialness of Jesus: early Christians coming from the background of monotheistic Judaism might believe God was acting in Jesus, but could they equate Jesus with God?

Yet John makes Jesus claim directly: 'The Father and I are one' (10.30). Many of the Christians for whom John wrote shared the ideas of the hellenistic world, where it was not unusual to think of a god as having a son (the Roman Emperors claimed to be sons of Zeus) or of a demigod (such as Bacchus) resulting from the union of a god (Zeus) and a human (Semele). John's more direct equation of Jesus with God would not sound strange to them but he wanted to say that the sonship of Jesus was unique, not the claim of any Mediterranean deity. How could he do justice to his belief that through Jesus a gracious God was establishing a new relationship with human beings despite their sin? He sees this as God's purpose from the creation, and so Jesus must have been with God in the creation, just as the Wisdom of God is seen to be with God in the beginning in Proverbs, the Wisdom of Solomon and Ecclesiasticus (it is instructive to compare John 1.1-14 with Ecclesiasticus 24.1-12). John knows that human beings can become sons and daughters of God through the actions of this 'son of God,' the one who can speak for his Father because he knows him so well. So he uses poetic language to express the mystery of how this can be: the Word, in Greek the *Logos*, has many rich connotations, affirming that the meaning of life is to be found in God and that God is revealed to us in Jesus.

Paul, writing much earlier than John, struggles with the same problem without calling Jesus God or identifying him with God: the emphasis is that Jesus 'is the image of the invisible God' and 'in him God in all his fullness chose to dwell' (Colossians 1.13-20).

On these attempts to express the wonder and mystery of God's relationship with humankind through Jesus, the early Church built the doctrine of the incarnation, the belief in the 'enfleshment' of God in the body of Jesus. That leaves us with many problems. Did Jesus have one nature or two? If he was God and so knew the end of the story, was his suffering real? If he was fully human in his temptations and in his suffering, was he God? And so the questions multiply. The definitions of the creeds were careful compromises designed to heal controversies of long ago in philosophical language that has lost much of its life and meaning, and they concentrated more on who Jesus was than on what he did or what he taught.

The Church has often failed to maintain the balance of its credal paradox that Christ is fully God and was fully man, usually emphasising his divinity at the expense of his humanity. It is a good corrective to focus more on the humanity Jesus shares with us, whose task is to create wholeness from the imperfection of our genetic inheritance and our parental upbringing, to grapple as he did with emotions like anger (Luke 11.37-52) and despair (Mark 14.32-36) and with temptations to be less than we are or are meant to be (eg Matthew 4.1-11). In this way I began to find a more real Jesus whose words and actions spoke to me.

But the incarnation is also a myth of subtlety and power. It tells of a God who abdicates his heavenly throne, gives up his power, to become one of us. Jesus was born in a stable to parents of no status; he rejected the temptation of kingly power (Matthew 4.8-10, Luke 4.5-8); he turned hierarchical ideas about power upside down, urging his followers to become servants one of another (eg Mark 9.30-37, 10.41-45). In Luke 22.24-30 Jesus says that the 'greatest' in God's kingdom, the one who shall be symbolically enthroned, is the servant. That a Jewish man should take up the role of servant usually reserved for women and slaves was revolutionary, undermining the norms of that patriarchal society, establishing a new model for relationships which renounced the use of power over others. Only a man who had the option of power could make that renunciation, one reason at least why Jesus needed to be male in gender. And he refused to go back on that renunciation even when threatened with death.

The Gospels use about one third of their space on the death and resurrection of Jesus. I found it hard to work out exactly what happened when, because the accounts differ, but the motives of the Jewish authorities were clear. They wanted to be rid of him because he threatened all they held sacred: he had attacked their leadership; cast doubt on the strict interpretation of the Law; taught that God favoured the poor above the rich and powerful; offered God's free forgiveness to all and underlined it by consorting with taxgatherers and sinners, with women and Samaritans. When Judas Iscariot gave them an opportunity, they acted swiftly because the business had to be concluded before the feast of the Passover. The charge that he was the Messiah could not be proved: Jesus neither confirmed nor denied it, and the witnesses contradicted each other. To claim to be the Messiah was not a blasphemy in Jewish law and the penalty was not death. So they laid a charge of insurrection before Pontius Pilate, saying Jesus claimed to be the King of the Jews, though they knew that he had no such pretensions. Pilate's concern was to keep the peace in this difficult Roman province: he wanted no trouble with the Jews and no popular disturbances. The easiest way out of a tight corner was to condemn Jesus, even though he was not convinced that the charge was proved.

Why did Jesus collude with those who sought his death? He challenged the Jewish authorities; made it easy for Judas to know where he would be late at night, when in prudence he should have left Jerusalem before dusk; and offered no defence at his trial. Perhaps the parable of the wicked vine-growers provides a clue, not least because it is close to the passion narrative in the synoptic Gospels (Matthew 21.33-44, Mark 12.1-12, Luke 20.9-18): the son has no choice but to deliver his father's message, even though from the experience of earlier messengers he fears what the consequences may be; and the vinegrowers may choose to accept him and change their behaviour or to kill him. So Jesus must deliver the good news of the Kingdom of God, knowing that the Jewish leaders may kill him for it but hoping that others, the remnant of Israel as described by the prophets (eg Zephaniah 3.11-13), will hear and respond.

The role of the death of Jesus in salvation is covered in chapter 12, but what meaning might it have within the myth of the incarnation? What might it tell me about God? It tells of a God who does not resort to power even to save himself (Matthew 27.39-44, Mark 15.29-32, Luke 23.35-43), a God who is in our midst in the darkest hour of human need, a God who does not shrink from the world's pain but who suffers with us. The myth goes beyond the death of one man in historical time to point to the reality that God is within the whole of human experience.

If Jesus is the human face of God
what God shows in his face?

A God who is vulnerable
Who suffers with us
and for us
Who lays down his power
so that he may love
to the end of his endurance
Who accepts the projection
of my rage and hate and guilt
so that I may recognise
what I have done
without self-righteous defence
and accept myself as I am
with a potential for good
if I acknowledge
my potential for ill
and the mixed motives
that inform all I do
Who leaves me free to choose
but offers grace and strength
if I am honest about myself
with myself and with God

if I seek to do
what with the whole of my being
I know I must

So what need was there for the resurrection? The writers of the New Testament believed that Jesus rose from the dead. In 1 Corinthians 15.3-9, written about 55 CE, Paul indicates that many early Christians believed that they had seen the risen Jesus. What did they see? We cannot know, but Jesus' followers changed: dazed and grieving after the crucifixion and lying low in their fear and disappointment, they burst into joyful and powerful action in Jerusalem, with Peter preaching at Pentecost about the risen Jesus (Acts 2.22-24) and many responding (2.37-47). Had they seen visions, more powerful experiences perhaps than the sense that we often have in grief that the dead are present with us? It is perhaps best to avoid speculation, particularly about a revived corpse or a resurrection body.

On Good Friday
darkness fell over the whole land
the sun's light failed
and the curtain of the Temple was torn in two
Then Jesus gave a loud cry
Father, into your hands I commend my spirit
and with these words he died
The crowd went home beating their breasts

It was the end
But after the sabbath
the women went to do what they could
for the body in the tomb
and awoke to a new reality
on Easter Day
Mary of Magdala had known him well

perhaps best of all
and she became alive to his presence

It was a new dawn

If an archaeologist found the bones of Jesus, would the resurrection be disproved? If I believed in the resurrection as a supernatural event whose reality depended on an empty tomb and if my case for Christianity depended upon the resurrection, I might be in trouble. Many have tried to prove that the event happened as written in the Gospels, but the accounts are not consistent one with another and the evidence for a supernatural event is sufficient only for a verdict of unproven. But modern historians go beyond asking whether what is written is true in any objective sense: what purpose did the writing serve for the writer and the reader? I had many questions. Do these stories testify that Jesus inspires us to change our lives and to embrace new ways of loving and forgiving, of caring and sharing? Does not a myth of dying and rising again like green growth from buried seed express powerfully the experience of repentance and new life (John 3.1-8), especially in a culture which believed in the resurrection of the body after death? What better symbols than the metaphors of human encounter could give voice to such a spiritual experience? Or do the stories assert that the love which accepts death as the cost is not in vain? Is the myth of dying and rising again a strong way of communicating the belief that despite all appearances evil does not triumph over love?

I have to live with my questions and stay with the stories without reading more into them than they will bear and without stifling my doubts in the hope that they will go away. Moving away from literal interpretations and bringing my imagination to bear on the stories, I ponder them in my heart rather than analyse them in my mind and the Jesus who walks beside me incognito on the Emmaus road (Luke 24.13-35) is able to make the myth come alive for me.

CHAPTER 12

BEING SAVED

At college I came to Christ, finding forgiveness for my sins through his death on the cross. A burden was lifted, but the effect dwindled as I became increasingly unhappy with the theology which described the experience: sin is breaking God's law; God's wrath and justice require that offenders are brought to judgement, to receive a just sentence from a righteous God; but a loving God sent his son to die on the cross, suffering the punishment we merit so that God could account us righteous.

At first my doubts centred on the 'how' of salvation: there must be a better way than a penal substitutionary atonement. God had rejected the sacrifice of Isaac (Genesis 22) and the best of the Old Testament believed that God did not want sacrifice (eg 1 Samuel 15.22, Psalm 51.16-17, Isaiah 1.10-16). Yet sacrifice featured largely in the New Testament, especially in Hebrews and Romans. Romans has other metaphors to describe the atonement such as liberation (3.24), renewed access (5.2), reconciliation (5.11), emancipation from slavery (6.17-18) and new life (8.9-11), and these are echoed in other books (eg 2 Corinthians 5.18-21, Colossians 1.21-22). But the most telling evidence against sacrificial theories is the picture Jesus drew of God. His God is not a wrathful king whose justice requires the sacrifice of his son, but a loving parent who runs to meet his repenting son (Luke 15.11-32), who rejoices to find a lost sheep (Matthew 18.12-14).

Perhaps the 'how' bothered me less than the 'why'. If God were loving, why was the sacrifice of Jesus needed? If God were angry or just, why was that anger or justice satisfied by the death of Jesus? If his death did satisfy God, would such a God merit my allegiance? Anger and love seemed to be at war in the being of God but I knew that there was no anger in God (see chapter 5).

I looked more closely at what Jesus said and did about sin. He seemed less worried about sinners than about those who condemn them (eg John 7.53-8.11). He braved disapproval to befriend sinners (eg Matthew 9.10-13, Luke 19.1-10), knowing that the 'poor in spirit' accept forgiveness more readily than those who believe themselves better than others (Luke 18.9-14). He reserved his strongest words (Matthew 23, Luke 11.37-54) for the pharisees, good people in terms of the Law but blind to their need of forgiveness for failing to respond to love's demands. More evil comes from goodness gone wrong (because we forget our potential for evil) than from more honest and obvious 'sinning'. Perhaps that is why Jesus made little use of the word 'sin' (nine times, if we allow for parallel accounts). Paul used it over ninety times, and the Church has sometimes focussed more on the problem of sin and less on the love of the forgiving and welcoming God depicted by Jesus.

So I rejoiced that Jesus put God's love at the centre of what he taught about sin and salvation. He turned the Mosaic Law on its head: it is not the outward fulfilling of the Law which counts in the kingdom of God, but the intention which underlies the action. He condemned anger and lust to the extent that if a part of the body offends we should cut it off (Matthew 5.21-30). To read it literally - and few do, for not many of a sound mind mutilate themselves - is to miss the point. Jesus used vivid language to show how anger and lust may stop us loving and accepting love; how anger unresolved may destroy our relationships and our personality; how as men and women we cannot relate honestly and fruitfully if we regard each other primarily as sex objects. We need to deal openly with our anger, lest we bury it in our subconscious and either project it onto others (so that they express it for us or use it against us) or turn it in on ourselves (so that we feel it as depression or anxiety). Likewise if we repress our lustful thoughts, we may project them onto others, so that we harm them by our self-righteous condemnation, make puritans of ourselves, and reduce our ability to love ourselves and others.

All of us have a shadow - the Church named it original sin and uses the Hebrew myth of the Fall (Genesis 3) to show the potential for evil which exists in all of us. But we are not responsible for the emotions we find in our shadow, for most originate in childhood experiences over which we had no control. We are however responsible for what we do with them, and the Old Testament tells stories that show what happens when our feelings run away with us (eg Genesis 37). We risk losing control when we hide the truth about ourselves from others and from ourselves, for then we may be taken unawares by an impulse contrary to the person we pretend to be. If we evade such an impulse, we should still be mindful of our potential for evil: there but for the grace of God... If we succumb, we should not blame the devil, for our devil is more likely to be the projection of what we find unacceptable in us than a kind of anti-God who tempts us. Facing our shadow is hard, for it usually contains the characteristics we most dislike in other people.

Jesus knew that if 'being good' is our primary aim, we would go wrong like the pharisees and deny our shadow's existence. So his standards were not impossibly high. Translating Matthew 5.48 (AV) as 'Be ye perfect, even as your Father in heaven is perfect' does little justice to the Greek: *teleios* may mean spotless when used of a sacrifice but when used of people it connotes maturity, completion and fulfilment. We might offer a translation like: 'Become whole people...' Wholeness requires us to own our shadow, acknowledge and feel its negative emotions, so that love may transform them into creative energy. The kingdom of God which Jesus proclaimed sets no conditions of goodness for entry. We may enter as we are, openly and honestly admitting what lies in our shadow, because God loves us as we are. That is the good news that Jesus taught and it came alive for me one day as I meditated on the parable of the prodigal son (Luke 15.11-32). This is what I wrote to share with others:

This beautiful story touches the roots of our tenderness and compassion. We respond to the pathos in the prodigal's misadventures. We might criticise the father for giving his younger son his share of the family estate - a wise father might have known that his son was not to be trusted with money but Jesus emphasises the father's joyous reception of his penitent son. Having (in the AV's fine phrase) 'wasted his substance in riotous living', the prodigal ends up looking after pigs, the lowest job of all for a Jew who regards pigs as ritually unclean. He comes to his senses: he has not been true to himself, his father or his God. He resolves to return home with words of repentance on his lips: 'Father, I am no longer fit to be called your son.' While he is a long way off, his father sees him and runs to meet him. Brushing aside the words of repentance he calls for a celebration, 'for this son of mine was dead and has come back to life; he was lost and is found.'

Yet the story is about a father and two sons: 'There was once a man who had two sons.' Identifying with the prodigal may make us gloss over his elder brother: we may not like to see ourselves in him. But the context (Luke 15 opens with disapproval of the scribes and pharisees: 'this fellow welcomes sinners and eats with them') suggests the parable was aimed at the righteous. The righteous are those who stay with God, as the elder son did with his father. Like the elder son they have a big investment in the Law. Jewish law gave the eldest son a double portion (Deuteronomy 21.17): when there were two sons, the elder would receive two thirds; and if a father made a gift of property in his lifetime, the capital became the son's but the father kept the income until his death. The parable depicts the position correctly: 'all that I have is yours,' but the elder son has no income from it - he depends on his father even for a kid to celebrate with his friends. Anger lies behind 'I never once disobeyed your orders.' His faithfulness has had scant reward. Again we might criticise the father: he might have guessed his elder son's feelings and rewarded his loyalty or at least sent to tell him of his brother's arrival. But the elder son is hurt that his good-for-nothing brother is so willingly forgiven and rewarded - genuine hurt often lies behind the self-righteousness which the pious may display towards forgiven sinners. When the elder son refuses to join the celebration, his father does respond with understanding. Just as he ran out to meet his younger son, so now he leaves the party to find his hurt and angry elder son. His words are intended to soothe and to explain. Just as he forgives the obvious sinning of the younger son, so he forgives the elder's self-righteousness.

So the parable of the prodigal son is badly named: it is the parable of a father's love for his two sons. Jesus intended us to see God in the forgiving father who rejoices at the prodigal's return; to recognise in the prodigal a sinner like the taxgatherers and prostitutes; to recognise in his elder brother the scribes and pharisees, horrified that their investment in the law was devalued when tax extortion and debauchery could be so easily forgiven. And yet God goes out to both.

Can we take the story further? Can we retell it as a parable of a mother's love for her two daughters? It could not be set in first century Palestine, because married women did not own property and few then could conceive how a mother's love might help our imaging of God. But if all of us are to identify with the story, we have to move it to our time, so that women can play each of the roles in it: like all good stories this story is about ourselves and the characters represent parts of ourselves. We might ask, as we might in interpreting a dream, which part of us is the younger, which the elder daughter or son, which the mother or father?

Transactional analysis suggests that this might be a good way forward. Each of us has a child within, usually fixed at a certain age and stage of development. We also internalise our parents or what our childish understanding made of them. As we grow to adulthood, the child and the parent can interfere with what we do as adults. Let us imagine that the child within is the prodigal, needing to escape parental control, rightly wanting to play but lacking the discipline and discernment to play safely. So things go wrong, and we need the adult in us - the father or mother in the story to rescue us, bandage our wounds, comfort us and welcome us back into the family. The adult enjoys the venturesome spirit and welcomes the trust of the child. But the child has to face the anger and disapproval of the parent - the elder brother or sister. Some of that anger is based upon resentment: 'I was never allowed to do that when I was your age.' But much of the anger and resentment is directed at the adult, for the adult encourages the child to explore, express feelings as they arise, be honest, open and vulnerable, grow into her or his own person; and the adult forgives the child's mistakes, loving the child for the child's sake, for being the child, not for doing what the parent wants. Parents often love conditionally (I'll love you, if...) but adults know love is unconditional: being good or bad does not count in the scale of adult loving. The adult finds it easier to love the spontaneous, impulsive child or even the fearful, damaged child than to love the disapproving parent who censures the child's honest but maybe socially unacceptable reactions. Yet the point of the story is that the adult goes out to both, accepts both, loves both, sets both free, for both have been imprisoned, the child by the confining rules of the parent, and the parent by its jealousy of the child's freedom.

Another line of interpretation is suggested by Jungian psychology. Let us imagine that the prodigal is our shadow, that part of us which shame makes us hide from others, which contains our potential for evil and the negative emotions that we refuse to acknowledge. Perhaps the elder brother or sister is our super-ego, the censor who forbids disclosure of the contents of our shadow, who pretends to be good so that he or she will be worthy of love, whose rage is for the most part hidden unless expressed as righteous anger, whose negative feelings tend to be projected onto others so that the conscious ego experiences them as the hostility of other people. So the censor is outraged when the prodigal shadow returns to be warmly welcomed by the father or mother. The father or mother is the greater self, not the conscious ego who designs the mask with which we face the world and polishes our persona. This greater self embraces the conscious and unconscious, knows what is best for us, strives to integrate all the aspects of our personality into a coherent whole, and tells the truth about us in the coded language of our dreams by day and night. This self has the capacity to embrace the returning prodigal with joy and forgiveness, to love us as we are for what we are. And that love can persuade the censor to lay down the cloak of self-righteousness: if we are loved we do not need to justify ourselves, to pretend to be better than we are, to bolster our self-esteem by looking down on others. We are lovable because we are loved. We need not use our energy to conceal who we really are from ourselves and others: we can use it for more positive ends. We are released by love into love.

Because God loved me unconditionally, I was released from the 'slavery of sin' (Romans 6.17-23): I need no longer fear that I might be found out and punished or that I might not be 'good enough'. Goodness was no longer my aim, though it might be a by-product of my feeling loved and of my loving. Salvation lay in love and forgiveness offered, accepted and experienced. My sin was not the sum of my acts of wrongdoing, nor even the complex of the impulses, desires and feelings of which I was ashamed, but acting contrary to the demands of love upon me, going against the grain of my true being, avoiding what my higher self knew was good for me or what God willed for me. But how might I discern these things when my shadow was so good at colluding with the evil within my family and community and when so much of my being lay hidden within the unconscious?

The answer lay in judgement. Jesus did not come to judge us, in the legal sense of passing a sentence of punishment on us for the 'sins' we have committed (John 3.17, 8.15, 12.47). But we do come under judgement, if John rightly interprets Jesus (John 12.47-48). The Greek word John uses for judgement is *krisis*, whose root means separating out or discriminating between. Frances Young suggests in *Face to Face* that judgement is the revealing of what we really are: Jesus does not judge us but he leaves us to judge ourselves when we come face to face with him, when we encounter loving kindness in others, when we meet suffering. We come to know who we really are, often suddenly and dramatically in our conscious selves, but more slowly and uncertainly in our unconscious.

Frances Young speaks movingly of how a handicapped child may be a judgement, a *krisis* discriminating between those who can work with the handicap and those who cannot. I am disturbed by handicap and I used to condemn myself for that, but it is not a moral issue and no one else was condemning me. So I could admit how I felt and once admitted my feelings were less threatening: I could work with them, through them, or even around them, and learn to enjoy helping with Riding for the Disabled. If I had hidden my feelings, I might have tried to help, failed and blamed my failure on circumstances or the disabled riders. Then I would never have come to terms with what I felt and I would have been less than by the grace of God I now am. What really matters is not whether we can or cannot cope but whether we are honest with ourselves and others about what we feel, whether we accept the judgement as the revelation of what we are like, and whether we repent, changing direction towards the love which can redeem us and transform our negative emotions into creative energy. Both Zacchaeus (Luke 19.1-10) and the prostitute (Luke 7.36-50) faced their own *krisis* and repented.

Honesty is not easy. Parental upbringing, social convention and religious teaching make us unwilling to expose what we really feel and our inner censor tries to conceal our negative emotions from other people and from ourselves. Spiritual direction, psychotherapy and counselling encourage us to be honest about ourselves, to face the *krisis* and repent from the depths of our unconscious being as well as in our conscious mind. But guilt seemed to prevent me from accepting the *krisis* and letting it penetrate into my unconscious.

Like many depressed people I felt guilty about many things. Some had a foundation in reality (my colleagues were burdened with extra duties), but many did not: who was I letting down by failing to be the best that anyone could be at my job? Because I could not be the best, I felt worthless. A simple piece of therapy showed me how excessive my guilt feelings were. Margaret was asked to pull me up whenever I used the words 'ought', 'should' and 'must', so that I could examine who or what within me uttered those words and either rephrase what I had said as 'I wish...' or reject it outright. Slowly I began to see how harmful my guilt was and how it had arisen from the injunctions of parents, teachers and preachers imposed on me in childhood. Guilt accused me of being a bad person, causing me to hide what I had done, thought or felt and to present a better but false face to others and to myself, in order to ward off the internalised anger or disapproval of those powerful people from my past. I feared that they would not love me, and I could not love myself because I did not meet their standards. My guilt had an unprofitable bedfellow called shame, the fear that what I had done, thought or felt might be exposed and that others would not love me as a result.

My meditation on the parable of the prodigal son should have set my guilt and shame at nought. If I were convinced that I was loved and forgiven whatever I had done and whatever were my innermost thoughts and feelings, I should be able to face the *krisis* which would show me as I was. But guilt and shame created a downward spiral:

Because I feel guilty
I must have sinned
Because I have sinned
I should feel guilty
Because I feel guilty
I should be punished
Because I have been punished
I was right to feel guilty
And so on
down the spiral

Despite the flawed logic, my guilt and shame paralysed me and stopped me feeling remorse. Remorse is the healthy sadness we feel when we have offended or hurt another or when we have failed to live up to the best that we can be, and it encourages us to accept the *krisis*, seek forgiveness and make what restitution we can. The paralysis seemed to block the way into the unconscious where the *krisis* needed to do its cleansing.

How might the blockage be removed? Despite my reservations about the atonement as a transaction whereby God's righteous anger at our sin is somehow satisfied by Jesus' death, might another interpretation of his death help? In the death of Jesus was God accepting responsibility for what had gone wrong in God's world? How might that work? I could understand how the way Jesus taught and lived his truth led to his death, but not why he refused to defend himself against the accusations made against him: he accepted the pain of an unjust and cruel death, he accepted the evil projected onto him by those who condemned him and carried out the sentence - and he forgave them (Luke 23.32-34). Perhaps defending himself would have reinforced the self-righteousness of those involved. Maybe he wanted them to reach their own *krisis*, accept their responsibility and feel his forgiveness. Could the death of Jesus be a myth conveying to the depths of our being that we can accept our share of responsibility for the evil of the world knowing we can be forgiven; that we can be true to our higher self, even if we are misunderstood, suffer and die, knowing that our acceptance of the evil of others in forgiveness and love destroys the evil? The resurrection seemed to say that love triumphs over evil despite appearances to the contrary. Love freely given and truly accepted can transform the least promising of situations.

Could I make the myth my own, or even remake it in metaphors of my own? Could it alter the way I felt in the depths of my unconscious? Could it remove the barrier of guilt and shame that cut me off from God? Could it transform the negative and destructive effects of internalised parental authority and family fear? As I struggled with these questions a picture came into my mind and stayed with me for many weeks:

I stand tall
on the white sand
The sun is overhead
in the clear blue sky
and it casts no shadows
The light is bright
but does not dazzle
The horizon does not shimmer
in the heat
for the noon sun is cool
like the moon

I am here

without knowing the route
by which I have come
There are no footsteps
to show my track across the sand
There is no road
to indicate the way I should go

I am here
Before
I would have preferred
the coolness of a woodland glade
to sun and sand
but this sun gives light
not shrivelling heat
and this sand is soft
not harsh desert sand
I am here
I am placed here
by the will and agency
of a mysterious other
I know I am safe
The vast open space speaks
of possibility
I can choose where to go
without fear of being lost

I am here
in a wilderness
a wild free place
saved from the shadow
of fear and tyranny
liberated from the guilt

which hides in the shade
from the light of the sun
and even of the moon
But the light has overcome the dark
and cast its shadows away

I am here
standing tall and fearless
in my wilderness
waiting
reflecting
pondering
before I set out
for the promised land
I do not know
where it lies
or which way to go
but I know I am safe
while I wait for a sign
not for the wind
the earthquake or the fire
but for the faint murmuring sound
which will arise
from the depths of my being

This vision was the unblocking, the breaking down of the barrier, which assured me that the punitive images of God that had inhabited my unconscious were being replaced; that I was being freed from the weight of guilt and shame; that the light was overcoming the darkness within and there would be light, or perhaps enlightenment, in whatever darkness there might be in the future; that the contents of my shadow were being transformed into more positive feelings and creative energy, for use in the new life which was about to begin. I had received a gift, the gift of salvation.

Salvation is a gift (Ephesians 2.8-10). Love and forgiveness are always gifts: they are not conditional on good behaviour. If they are made conditional, they are frauds, being used as weapons in a power game. And they are free gifts, imposing no obligations. Preaching that threatens us with the dire results of sin, that plays on our guilt or fear, cannot bring us to a saving knowledge of love and forgiveness: a wrathful God and eternal damnation are not good news. Such preaching creates an idol which reinforces our fear and guilt and makes us unable to face the *krisis* that enables us to have an honest relationship with ourselves, with others and with God. Honesty permits the receiving, sharing and giving of love. The good news is that God loves us even before we know our need of God's love.

Yet, though our salvation is a gift, we have to work at it, to open up all the layers of our personality to forgiveness and love, for what we say with our lips (and consciously believe we mean) may not be what we feel in our unconscious, which may bring our loving intentions to nought. We have to keep bringing our guilt and shame to the *krisis* that reveals their true nature, so that the truth of what we are, the bad as well as the good, may be loved, forgiven and transformed. No one can do this work for us: we cannot avoid it by surrendering who and what we are to the Church and letting the Church tell us who and what we should be. We have to work out our own salvation in fear and trembling (Philippians 2.12-13).

Salvation is a spiritual gift: it does not ensure our health, wealth or success. Indeed it may make us uneasy about wealth and success. For although salvation is individual, it is only effective in community. The test of salvation is how we respond to the demands of love upon us: this is the point of the parable of the sheep and the goats (Matthew 25.31-46). It might be better if, like the sheep, we did not know that we were saved, for we might be less tempted to think ourselves better than those who have not yet recognised the gift offered to everyone. The parables of the labourers in the vineyard (Matthew 20.1-16) and the unmerciful servant

(Matthew 18.23-35) teach that no one can claim a privileged relationship with God or feel superior to any other human being. Because we all need God's forgiveness and love, the only safe response when we meet wrongdoing in another is to forgive and love the wrongdoer.

This is not to be soft on wrongdoing. It is to be realistic, for it removes the sense of superiority which encourages us to punish the wrongdoer not only for his or her own admitted or detected wrongdoing but also for the wrongdoing we have committed - even if only in mind. Projecting our faults onto others is very destructive, causing our society to create policies which punish rather than rehabilitate offenders; penalise the poor as shiftless, shirking or even wicked rather than see them as victims of circumstance or of other people's greed; reward the rich as if they were virtuous or specially favoured by God. Accepting God's love for us challenges us to respond in love to the needs of others, and that challenge may require much more of us than the effort of being good.

Jesus pointed out how we may fail to achieve salvation for ourselves because we do not respond to those in need. The good Samaritan is the best known parable with this message (Luke 10.31-46), but his attitude to wealth is also instructive. Jesus was not against wealth, for he enjoyed being entertained by his wealthy friends, but the parables of Dives and Lazarus (Luke 16.19-31) and the rich fool (Luke 12.16-21) and his encounter with the rich young man (Matthew 19.16-26, Luke 18.18-27) show how wealth may keep us rooted in the way things are rather than stimulate us to think how we might work towards a more just society. Wealth may not be our problem: there are other false gods like work, study or pleasure, even good works or religion!

Salvation is not only from those false gods but is also into the kingdom of God: we may have to lose our former life in order to find a new life in the kingdom, a new life of such quality that we describe it as eternal. That life begins with the experience of being loved and forgiven. From that experience may come the will, the courage and the energy to work for the coming of God's kingdom and to face the daunting challenges of our suffering world.

Chapter 13

MAKING SENSE OF SUFFERING

Some time after leaving my job I felt the need for something tangible to commemorate the years I had spent at the college. I thought I would like a cross. After some searching we found a silver cross and Margaret bought it for me. On the back we had inscribed with the college's name and the dates I had been there. I wear it a lot, particularly when I feel under threat from the witches that inhabit my personal mythology. At one of the clergy workshops I was asked why I was wearing it. I explained why we had bought it and, to my surprise, went on to say that the past few years had been a kind of crucifixion. This came to me as a sort of revelation. Throughout my depression I had been conscious of the dark and of the pain, but I had not thought of myself as suffering. I had even spent many hours wrestling with the problem of suffering but on Danny's behalf, not my own. Perhaps it was safer to do the wrestling at one remove.

On Easter Day
I wrote a poem about Good Friday
because that is where we are
all of us who love Danny
standing at the foot of a cross

The logic in us knows
that terminal means he will die
but most of our being does not hear
does not want to hear
'his illness is at an advanced stage'
Then we see how his struggle for breath
is becoming harder and harder
and we can no longer deny the reality
that his death will come
perhaps soon
perhaps after his brave spirit
has rallied his frail body once more
but we know now
that terminal means he will die

I want to rage at the dying of the light
I hammer on the doors of heaven
Why? Why?
Though I know there is no answer
to the mystery of suffering
I want to understand
for it might then be easier to bear
the suffering of this dear young child

Daniel died two months later, months I found hard to bear. I struggled to make sense of all the suffering and this is how I came to define the problem:

It is no answer to talk
of God's higher purposes
We may only see through a glass darkly

or glimpse puzzling reflections in a mirror
but unmerited suffering can have no place
in the purposes of a loving God
nor is it constructive to see
suffering as a punishment for sin
either mine or another's
for a loving God forgives
Either God is not loving
or he is not powerful
If he can pull the strings
to end unnecessary suffering
and does not
he is not loving
and some would say
if he cannot pull the strings
he is not God

Many Christians hold the paradoxical belief that God is all-powerful and all-loving, and some urged me to do the same, for truth may often be found by holding apparent opposites in tension. I tried to hold onto the belief in God's power, for God might answer my prayers for Danny, but I soon saw that such a belief would commit me to the view that God could prevent suffering but chooses not to, perhaps for loving reasons beyond our understanding. And I would still have to face the question: 'Why does God let this happen?' Perhaps all who suffer must ask this question, for it may help us to vent some of our anger on the one person who can take it - but is it the right question? There are two reasons why it may not be.

The first is the easier reason. Buddha's Four Noble Truths begin: 'All existence involves suffering.' Our mental suffering might be lessened if we could accept that life is difficult, often painful, frequently unfair, and suffering is part of it. Suffering is one of the mysterious 'givens' of life, one of the many mysteries that we cannot unravel. Our life with its joys and sorrows is a gift, and seeing our good fortune as a gift, not a right, may put our suffering into perspective. Achieving such a perspective is hard, for we do not readily give up our search for an explanation. Perhaps, like Job, all who suffer must ask 'why me?'

Suffering is not God's gift in any direct sense, for God does not will or cause suffering: such an intention is not compatible with the loving God revealed in the life and teaching of Jesus. God may use suffering and bring good out of it, but that is a different matter, as we shall see. Neither does it help to regard the devil as the cause of suffering. The devil is not some sort of anti-God stalking the earth to tempt us into evil and to bring us suffering. The devil may play a part in the mythology which helps us to understand the shadow side of our unconscious or even the collective shadow in the collective unconscious but we need to integrate the shadow into our personality rather than to project it onto an external being whom we can blame for what we do not like in ourselves.

It is good that we need not take what the Bible says about the devil literally, for to do so makes the Book of Job less satisfactory than it may be. The prologue shows God allowing Satan to inflict great suffering upon Job to test his loyalty to God, but it was probably added when the ancient myth was written down in about the fourth century BCE. It is not essential to the story, for the myth centres on the dialogue between Job and his friends. At first Job responds to his suffering with

Naked I came from the womb,
naked I shall return whence I came.
The Lord gives and the Lord takes away;
blessed be the name of the Lord. (1.21)

His friends come and 'for seven days and seven nights they sat beside him on the ground, and none of them spoke a word, for they saw that his suffering was very great' (2.13 - how rarely do we take time to sit silently beside those who suffer). Job curses the day of his birth, but his friends then urge the oldest explanation of suffering: it is a punishment for sin. Job protests his innocence: 'Let me know my offence and my sin. Why do you hide your face and treat me as your enemy?' (13.23-24). God is angry with the three friends: 'Unlike my servant Job, you have not spoken as you ought about me' (42.7). Had they chosen the wrong explanation? Finally Elihu points out that God is so much higher than mere mortals that it is not for Job to question what God does, and then God speaks to Job 'out of the tempest' about his transcendent power (38-41). Finally Job submits himself to God:

I knew of you then only by report,
but now I see you with my own eyes.
Therefore I yield,
repenting in dust and ashes. (42.5-6)

This fine story is full of insight and, as we shall see later, contains one of the keys to the problem of suffering. Yet it is not wholly satisfying, partly because it depicts God playing with Job like a puppet on a string but mainly because it suggests that suffering is a punishment for the personal sin of the sufferer. Certainly suffering is often the result of sin, the failure to do what in the depths of our being we know is good for us and for others or to do the will of God. So we may bring suffering upon ourselves, in heart disease, ulcer or cancer. We may cause others to suffer through our carelessness, greed, anger, jealousy and the like. As a society we may create suffering by failing to meet the needs of the poor, the sick, the orphan or the prisoner. And so on. In such cases we can see the direct causal link between sin and suffering without importing the agency of God. But some suffering is in no sense the result of sin: there are accidents, chance happenings which cause death or injury but which bear no relation to the moral worth of the sufferer. The innocent suffer as often, perhaps more often, than the guilty: 'Why do the wicked live on, hale in old age, and great and powerful?' (Job 21.7). Such suffering makes nonsense of the notion that suffering is the just punishment for sin, although the afflicted may blame themselves for the suffering imposed upon them.

There are moral objections to suffering as a punishment for sin. If others believe that we must have sinned because we have fallen on hard times, they may oversimplify the complexities behind our moral choices and become self-righteous. Worse still they may draw the corollary, that their good fortune is God's reward for their good behaviour, moral superiority or strong faith. But God does not operate a morally dubious insurance scheme: 'behave well and I'll see you all right.' Such ideas may make us self-righteous about poverty: 'if only they worked as I do...,' so that our grasp on spiritual reality may be undermined by wealth and security. We do well to reflect on the hard words of Jesus: 'it is easier for a camel to pass through the eye of a needle than for a rich man to enter the kingdom of heaven' (eg Matthew 19.24). The gospel is biased to the poor, in material things as well as in spirit, because the poor know their need, but otherwise it is hard to believe that God has favourites: the Puritans were insufferable because they believed that they were God's elect.

But the overwhelming objection is theological. Jesus warned us not to attribute suffering to sin: if suffering resulted from sin, we would all suffer because we all sin (Luke 13.1-5). He showed that God's way of dealing with sin is forgiveness: God is a father who forgives (Luke 15.11-32), who goes out to seek and save the lost (Luke 15.1-7). His declaration of God's forgiveness healed the paralysed man (eg Mark 2.1-12). Because Jesus is God's self-revelation, we may place less weight on Old Testament passages like: 'I, the Lord your God, am a jealous God, punishing the children for the sins of the parents to the third and fourth generation of those that reject me. But I keep faith with thousands, those who love me and keep my commandments' (Exodus 20.5-6). This love-me-or-else God may well be the projection of our own sin and guilt.

Even then we are not finished with the causes of suffering, and this leads to the second reason why our question (Why does God let this happen to us?) may be inappropriate. One major cause of suffering lies in the random effects of unpredictable nature, the so-called acts of God, about which we might now say the only certainty is that they are not the acts of God. Pre-scientific people may have attributed storm, flood, drought, earthquake, volcano and other natural disasters to the anger of God, but we have no need to do so, for we can go a long way towards explaining how they happen. We daily understand the natural law more fully, so that it makes less and less sense to assume that God interferes in its operation. Some still say that God can and does, but it is hard to obtain objective evidence of such activity. Healings that sometimes follow prayer and miracles that seem to bend the natural law are not proof of divine activity, because it is hard to establish a causal link between them and God, and those who see God's activity in them usually will not admit evidence that might falsify their belief. So we are best to avoid attributing to God any physical phenomena that we cannot yet explain, for all we do is to shrink the relevance of God as science comes to understand more about the laws of nature. The nineteenth century conflict between Christianity and science suggests that it is Christianity which is the loser when it moves outside the spiritual realm: 'God is spirit and those who worship him must worship in spirit and in truth' (John 4.24).

So perhaps we need to be honest and say that God cannot avert the earthquake; alter the split-second timing which makes the difference between an accident and a lucky escape; undo the mistakes in our upbringing which cause us pain in later life; or stop the terminal disease from running its course. A pretty useless God, you may say. But wait!

Job finds no explanation for his suffering, no answer to the mystery of its existence, but he finds relief from suffering when he comes into the presence of God and recognises that God is with him in his suffering. God is in the earthquake, God is in the car crash, God is in the cancer,

God is in the handicap - whatever our suffering, God is in it with us. The writer of Psalm 139.7-12 clearly believes that, and Jesus on the cross reveals God in the heart of suffering and shows God's grief for the suffering in the universe.

The myth of the incarnation means
God is in it with us
sharing our joys and sorrows
It does not mean
that death shall have no dominion
that we can triumph over death
as if it had no reality
It is real enough
as you and I know
and God cannot alter it
God does not want your submission
nor even your resignation to his will
He does not mind if you doubt him
if you accuse or even curse him
He knows it may relieve your sorrow
And he weeps with you
for he is in the experience with you
He has died himself
and has watched his son dying
By accepting what he could not change
he transformed it
making the desolation bearable

The 'you' in this extract from a longer poem is Victor Hugo whose impassioned poem *A Villequier* I read when Danny was dying (see chapter 9). It helped me to see that God was in the suffering surrounding Danny's death. God was with us, working in us and through us to bring good out of the suffering through the power of love. Gerald Priestland used to say that God's only power is the power of love-in-the-form-of-grace, and that is a mighty power, as the resurrection testifies. The resurrection myth is the nearest that Christianity gets to an explanation of suffering, and then the emphasis is more on the outcome than the cause. Jesus saw himself in the role of the Suffering Servant 'by whose wounds we are healed' (Isaiah 53.5). By accepting suffering and death, Jesus overcame death.

We see nature renewing itself through the cycle of birth, growth, pain, death and rebirth: the seed dies to give birth to new life and the animal passes on its genes to the next generation before it dies. But we seem unwilling to accept nature's way for ourselves: we think that the life that must continue is our own conscious life rather than our genes. Yet we all have to die, and acceptance of the inevitable removes our fear and enables us to live what remains to us with joy. What the resurrection myth seems to say is that the pattern of the natural cycle works for the spirit: our spiritual life can be renewed following suffering and death. Our suffering is a kind of death - sometimes the actual death of a loved one, or the death of health, wealth or happiness - and it is only when we have come to terms with that death, that we can rise again to new life. And we do that through love.

There is a mystery about God
and a mystery about suffering
and the key to both is love

The wisdom from the depths holds out hope
the hope that we shall be made whole
that we shall be healed
from the anguish of our tumultuous emotions
from our fear anger guilt and grief
That healing is wrought from and by love

the love which looks horror in the face
and still goes on loving
the love which finds joy in service
and inspires joy in the served
Such joy transforms suffering
and brings the true healing of acceptance
far better than the miracle cure
that may buy some months of bodily existence
without healing the mind and spirit

Love-in-the-form-of-grace means love as a free gift, a gift which does not depend on our merits but on our need. It does not explain the mystery of suffering, but it enables those who accept the gift to live with the mystery, to find a saving possibility in every situation, to accept and work through the suffering. God's love can transform tragedy. It can bring joy out of sorrow and hope out of despair.

Accepting the gift of love when we are suffering is hard, especially for those who have been taught to be self-reliant and self-contained. But suffering is always a judgement. It is not a judgement in the sense of condemnation: we have seen that suffering is not a punishment for our wrongdoing. But it is a *krisis* (see chapter 12), a revealing of who we really are. We may not like what we find. It is hard for a strong man to cry or to accept that he feels as defenceless as he did as a small boy. It is hard for a loving woman to express her anger. But we do need to know what we are feeling, to be honest about the emotions which well up within us and spill out of us. It may take some time before we can even name what we are feeling, let alone express it, and we may need help in order to do so. We may need people to sit with us, to hold us in the way that a good parent comforts a child. We may need the wise counsel of those that have been through the experience before us, of those who are able to listen and to reflect back to us what we are saying so that we can hear it ourselves. We may need the reassurance that we are not responsible for the emotions that arise within us, but only for what we do with them.

Job is so angry that he cannot see God, and we all have to cope with feelings of anger: 'why me?' It is all right to be angry. Our anger will not destroy as our two year old tantrums made us fear it might. We may be more angry than our suffering seems to warrant, because echoes from our past release from our unconscious anger felt but not expressed at the time. Whatever, we should allow ourselves to feel our anger, for if we suppress it, it may explode inappropriately at a later date or we may project it onto others. We should find safe ways of expressing it. We can be angry with God: by accepting the worst of men's anger and hostility on the cross Jesus showed that God can take it. God is not angry with Job, but perhaps Job's self-righteousness causes him to project his anger onto God. When Elihu challenges Job's self-righteousness and changes the focus away from the false explanation of his suffering and towards what God has done and can do, Job is able to hear God and to see that God has been with him all the time. In yielding to God Job does not admit that his friends have been right after all, but that his anger has given him a false perspective on his suffering and has cut him off from God. Now he feels remorse that his anger has impaired his vision and rejoices that he can see and feel God within his suffering. His restoration to position and wealth is not necessary, and in one sense it spoils the story, which may be a reason for thinking that it was not part of the original story on which the Book of Job was based. The real point is that Job is able to find the healing for his suffering in his relationship with the living God, without God needing to effect a miracle cure or to produce the happy-ever-after ending that a later editor added to the story.

We often need to work through our emotions before we can allow ourselves to feel the love offered to us when we are suffering. I have laboured the point about anger as an example, but there are other emotions which have to be worked through. Guilt is commonly felt by those who grieve ('if only I had...') but there may be a mix of undifferentiated emotions including sorrow, despair, anger, guilt, fear and anxiety. We have to find the courage to face our real feelings, to name them, to allow ourselves to feel them, to work through them patiently and persistently. We have to find the courage first, as I tried to explain to a friend who made an attempt on her own life:

In the end it's your choice
You can go on running
pursued
as you think
by the demons of your pain
Or you can screw up your courage
and turn to face them
And you will find
that God is in the pain
and God's love can bring joy out of sorrow
It will be a battle
often a hard battle
and you will need all your courage
It will take time
perhaps a long time
but each victory will bring
renewed strength for the next battle
and you will begin again
to respect and love yourself
for what you are

Ultimately it is the power of love that transforms, the gift which we receive because we are mothers, fathers, daughters, sons, wives, husbands, friends, because we are all children of God (1 John 4.7). Love is not earned: it is given freely and without condition. And love freely given and thankfully accepted has the power to bring good out of the most tragic situations. What is amazing is that there is so much love on offer, that in the midst of tragedy and horror love goes on loving. We shall not be able to turn the clock back, but there will be new life if we open ourselves to the love of God, so often expressed in the words and actions of those near to us.

From its miraculous beginnings in love
our life journeys towards
the mysterious fulfilment of love
in the creation of wholeness
in the healing of suffering
Can wholeness and healing be achieved
in so short a life?
Daniel had a wisdom beyond his years
accepting what must be
and finding joy in what might be
He gave more love than he received
and achieved more of real worth
in his four and a half years
than most of us manage
in three score years and ten
He was not cured
but he was healed and made whole
That may make it easier
to live with the mystery
of his early death
If we are made by love for love
will not love be sufficient
to face that ultimate mystery
Is not our end in our beginning?

Suffering undergone and redeemed through love healed Danny and looking back I can now see that my own suffering has been creative. While I was in the midst of it I would have done all I could to avoid it, but now that I have been loved through it, I know that I have learned so much that I would not change what has been. I have not found an explanation for suffering to satisfy my intellect, but love has enabled me to come to terms with what James Joyce called 'love's bitter mystery.' Through love I can live with that mystery and the sites of my wounds have become the seedbeds of new strengths. Like Paul I have come to know that nothing can separate us from the love of God (Romans 8.31-39).

CHAPTER 14

RELATING TO THE CHURCH

Do I dare
to leave the safety
of the battlemented church?
Can I climb from the crypt
leaving buried there
the ghosts of my past?
Shall I open the door
and venture a foot
on the yellow brick road
which leads through the meadow
towards the river of life?
Shall I walk tall
with never a backward glance
free from the chains
that have imprisoned me?

When I wrote this my feelings towards the Church were rather ambivalent, for I had projected my childhood feelings about my clerical father onto the Church, usually in its Anglican form. The onset of a depression usually marked a retreat from more active membership, though I have never severed all links. Recovery from this depression seemed to require me to undo that projection, to disentangle it from the real successes and failures of the Church. As I have taken back authority from my father and the Church (see chapter 3), I have found a way of living with the Church which I describe as being on the edge. I first defined it like this:

I stand on the edge of the Church, because I am both attracted and repelled by it. I am attracted by its founder and what he taught: I am repelled by some of the doctrines the Church has developed about him. I am attracted by its love, its prophecy, its wisdom: I am repelled by its power, its dogmatism and its self-righteousness. I am attracted by its invitation to go on the pilgrim road and repelled by its insistence that it alone knows the way. I am attracted by some of its symbolism and repelled by much of its language. I am attracted by some of its spirituality and repelled by the banality of much of its worship.

Recently I have met and corresponded with many who share this experience of being on the edge, uncertain whether to stay or to leave. Most express ambivalent feelings about the Church as an institution, and perhaps in our time this is how the Church has to be defined: I use Church with a capital C to mean the sum of the institutional churches, for most of us experience the Church through the institutions (the structures and practices) of our own particular church. But when Jesus called Peter the rock and said 'on this rock I will build my church' (Matthew 16.13-20), what did he intend? The Greek word used for church was *ecclesia,* the word classical Athens used for the assembly of all its freeborn male citizens. Jesus used it again in Matthew 18.17, where the REB renders it as the congregation. The risen Jesus told Peter to 'feed his sheep' (John 21.15-17), and sent his disciples to proclaim the gospel and baptise new believers (Matthew 28.19-20, Mark 16.15-16). In John Jesus commanded his followers: to wash one another's feet (13.2-17), love one another

(13.34-35, 15.11-17), trust God and him (14.1-14), obey his commands (14.15-26) and dwell in his love (15.1-10). Matthew 6.5-15 and Luke 11.1-13 give his teaching on prayer; 1 Corinthians 11.23-25 and some manuscripts of Luke (perhaps not the best - compare Luke 22.17-20 in the AV with the NEB or REB) record his command to commemorate the Last Supper.

Jesus spoke of himself as the vine and his disciples as the branches (John 15.1-6), but would he have recognised the New Testament metaphor for the Church, the body of Christ (eg Romans 12.4-10, 1 Corinthians 12.12-31, Ephesians 4.11-16)? What would he have made of bishops, elders (presbyters) and deacons (eg 1 Timothy 3.1-13, Titus 1.5-9)? We may think it strange, in view of the controversy over women priests, that the New Testament does not mention priests as office-holders in the Church, seeing the Church as the priesthood (eg 1 Peter 2.4-10). A bishop's functions in administering sacraments could be delegated to an elder, so that elders came to be seen as priests but not normally until the third century. Would Jesus have countenanced the power structure which was created when the Church became the official religion of the Roman Empire in the fourth century? And similar questions are thrown up by many other developments in the Church's history.

In its structure and worship the Church has gone beyond what Jesus laid down for his followers. How well do later traditions catch the spirit of the early Church (see Acts 2.41-47) and how far do they further the gospel of love and produce the fruits of the spirit? Though the Church has sometimes met criteria like these, it has often failed to meet them, and Christians have much to repent. So is the Church a failure, are its members hypocrites? I think not. Members try to follow the will of God, but they misunderstand or disobey and so fail and need forgiveness, as we all do. They deserve condemnation only if they pretend that they are better than non-members. Is there enough good to persuade us to stay? Or does the bad suggest we should leave?

Many who accept modern science and philosophy are unhappy that worship often still reflects biblical metaphysics. Some church leaders act as if recent (or even old!) theological thinking must be kept from the people in the pew, but theology - how we talk about God - is central to our faith and worship. Those who offer new ideas, challenge established thinking or express doubts often receive a hostile reception, as if church members cannot be trusted to think, as if any variation from orthodoxy threatens the whole fabric of belief. Perhaps the key issue is authority, in the Catholic and Anglican traditions at least. The clerical leadership uses 'top-down' and 'power-over' models of authority: God gives power through his son's commission to mostly male bishops and priests, excluding most worshippers from meaningful power and most women from positions of authority. Challenges to the status quo evoke great hostility: the ordination of women as Anglican priests threatens the male patriarchy that has ruled the Church for centuries.

To give up power is always hard
but only by resigning their power
can men be freed to love
as women
being powerless in the church
have always done
and it is only through love
that God is found and held

The ordination of women as priests is one among many issues of faith and morals on which liberal and radical views are under attack from the traditionalists and fundamentalists who seem to be winning a larger slice of a shrinking cake. Perhaps it is time to leave. Leaving is intellectually honest. We might conserve our energy for causes closer to the gospel than church politics. We might preserve our emotional well-being, for it is hard to express anger during a service or a sermon: we cannot say 'balderdash' out loud too often, and later objections cannot undo the effect of what has been said or done. Depression reduces our control over our feelings and so it may be wise to avoid services or sermons that may anger or upset us greatly. So why not leave?

In the first place it smacks of surrender. The case against the 'top-down' and 'power-over' models of authority must be argued. Leaving weakens the hand of those who stay to fight and ensures a traditionalist victory. It may be tempting to see the rise of traditionalism as evidence of the death throes of the Church and seek to hasten its death, so that a new Church may rise from the ashes of the old. Good theology perhaps, but poor history: the Church has survived many vicissitudes for nearly 2000 years and what we see as evidence of terminal decline may in reality be a defence mechanism helping the Church to cope with a period of rapid social change. We would be foolish to write off the Church prematurely. We should argue our case.

Secondly, leaving on my own makes little impact. To attract attention to my reasons for leaving means organising a splinter group with those of like mind. There are benefits in such a move: we may then organise and worship as we choose. In the past new churches have usually defined themselves by their differences from the main body of the Church, but time has brought both parties to recognise that common beliefs far outweigh those differences. This - and declining numbers - has motivated the growing ecumenical movement of the twentieth century. We shall be moving against the tide of history.

Thirdly, our leaving may cause such anger that we invest too much in the truth to which our separation bears witness, so that we let that truth fossilise into an idol and lose touch with the spirit of God which flies free. If our truth is to remain alive, we must live in the tension between opposite views. Can we live with integrity in that tension, without swinging to one pole or the other, so that we may find creativity and new life? Perhaps that is what living on the edge is about, living in the tension of being neither a full member nor an outsider, as I tried to explain in this poem:

Living on the edge of the Church
I am tolerated
patronised or even pitied
because I haven't seen the Light
and can't accept the Truth
of its teaching or tradition
But light can be a fire of love
or the blinding glare of a torture chamber
The light of the Church
has been both
is both
So I must choose
when to add my candle to that light
And truth can be a liberation
or an imprisoning straightjacket
The truth of the Church
has been both
is both
So I must choose
when to add my truth to that truth

Living on the edge of the Church
my candle is unseen
the whisper of my truth unheard
If my candle joins others
to make a warmer glow
the Church turns its face away
If my whisper becomes a shout
the Church closes its ears
Are my light and truth
so frightening
that they must be rejected

out of hand?
Are my questions so threatening
that they can't be entertained
for a moment?

Is the Church so blind and deaf
that it can see only its own art
hear only its own music?
How many bonfires must I light?
How many megaphones must I use?

Living on the edge of the Church
is dangerous
for bonfires can rage
out of control
and megaphones deafen
or seem to blow my own trumpet
Yet the light of truth
is a candle
which with other candles
dispels the dark
without destroying it
And the whisper of truth
arises from the depths of wisdom
and is easy to miss
in the din of shouting
If I can't make myself
seen or heard
without a raging fire
or a deafening shout
I risk destroying
what truth I have

Living on the edge of the Church
is dangerous
for if I draw near to the Church
and my light is not seen
and my truth not heard
I risk being absorbed
and buried with my truth
within the system of the Church
Then my candle no longer lights my way
and the whisper of my wisdom
no longer guides my step

Living on the edge of the Church
is lonely
It would be easier
to surrender my mind
to its teaching and tradition
I would then be accepted
and welcomed as a true son
I want to be accepted
but I cannot live a lie
I can only stand on the edge
until my candle lights my way
towards the centre
I can only stand on the edge
until my whispering wisdom
can make itself heard
within the Church
Maybe the Church will learn
to listen
Maybe I shall learn

to speak
in a more penetrating whisper
Until then
I must live my truth on the edge

Living on the edge is not easy. The comfort that the Church offers to full members may draw us in: how can we accept comfort without compromising our integrity? The inefficiency of the Church at the local level may tempt us to show that we can do it better, but at what cost? The Church may drive us away, seeing us as enemies of the 'full gospel,' as scapegoats to carry away the doubts that loyal believers cannot face. Retaliating against such projection will justify members in driving us away: accepting it may enable the Church to recognise its projection. So by living on the edge we may help the Church to come to a *krisis* which reveals what it is and what it is doing, so that it may move towards a more honest dialogue with its members and with those outside.

How can we maintain our spiritual and mental strength on the edge while weathering the protest and projection that insiders may throw at us? We may find support from kindred spirits in our local congregation but we may have to look further afield. Some of us find strength in a Quaker meeting which we attend while keeping our links with the local church. Others turn to one of the networks that are slowly being created. Kaleidoscope is a loose association centred on Norwich which seeks to explore faith from a liberal or radical perspective, and similar local networks exist elsewhere. SCM Trust has begun to build a national network and to stimulate local initiatives. Some years older than the SCM Trust is the Cairns Network, whose members have given thought to what a network might achieve.

Networks have the advantage over church institutions in that they have no formal structure and no hierarchy: the focus is on the people who are both the knots and the links of the net, making connections one with another. The metaphor of the net has limitations because it implies finite edges, but the edges need to be fuzzy, to encourage people in exploratory and creative thinking and discussion. So there will be no test of membership, although as time goes on members may clarify some values and concerns as the basis upon which further membership is invited. Essentially a network functions because people wish to share who they are and what they have learned, because they are prepared to trust and be trusted, to be vulnerable and supportive. A network may be a model for how the people of God might best function, but in the meantime it may help us to find companions on the way and to develop the soul-friendship that we need if we who live on the edge of the Church are to do their proper work for the Church. A strange and lovely happening made me think that work might be prophecy.

In the midst of depression I was finding it harder than ever to pray and a friend made me a sculpture to serve as a visual prayer (see chapter 15). Three biblical texts were inscribed around the base. As I looked them up one became alive for me, resonating with something deep within me: 'Before I formed you in the womb I chose you, and before you were born I consecrated you; I appointed you a prophet to the nations' (Jeremiah 1.5). I asked Jessica how she had chosen the texts and she said that after much prayer she felt guided to them. I was puzzled. Was I being called in the same way that Jeremiah was? Could I trust the strength of this feeling? What might it mean?

I turned for help to the prophets of the Bible. I found warnings against false prophets (eg Jeremiah 23.16-40, Ezekiel 13.1-9). True prophets are called by God to 'speak the words of the Lord' (eg Jeremiah 1.4-10, Ezekiel 2.1-5). Jesus said that we would recognise them by their fruit (Matthew 7.15-20), and Paul encouraged prophecy because it searches the conscience and lays the secrets of the heart bare (1 Corinthians 14.24). So a prophecy may be from God when its fruits are good and it enables the people of God to see themselves as they are. Was it possible that God was calling me and those like me who stand on the edge to speak 'the words of God' to the Church?

What might those 'words of God' be? The Hebrew prophets seem to foretell the future, but it may be that those who later set down their words gave their prophecy added weight by writing as if they had predicted the calamities with which they were wrestling. Early Christians searched the prophets for texts foretelling Christ, often taking texts out of context, as Matthew did with Isaiah 7.14: the child to be born as a sign to Ahaz that Judah would be saved was more probably his son Hezekiah than Jesus born centuries after his death. Christians since have devised ingenious schemes seeking to prove that the prophets foretold many events in history, and some have argued that fulfilled prophecy validates the authority of scripture. But the significance of the prophets lies less in prediction than in pointing to the *krisis* created by the disasters which befell Israel. The prophets tended to see those disasters as God's punishment for the people's sins, though they also bore witness to the tender and merciful qualities of God (eg Isaiah 43.1-7, Jeremiah 31.3-6, Ezekiel 34.11-16, Micah 7.18-20). We now set the life and teaching of Jesus against the notion that suffering is a punishment for sin (see chapters 12 and 13). Prophecy succeeded when its hearers could not avoid the truth: it succeeds now when we accept judgement.

The prophets said that God was grieved, exasperated and angry because the people of Israel had broken their side of the covenant (eg Isaiah 24.5, Jeremiah 11.10, Hosea 8.1). Their actions showed that they no longer cared for the ways of the Lord, worshipping idols (eg Isaiah 44.9-20, Habakkuk 2.18-20); following false gods and false prophets (eg 1 Kings 18.17-40, Zephaniah 1.4-6); performing empty rituals (eg Isaiah 58.1-14, Amos 5.21-27, Micah 6.6-8); oppressing the poor and weak (eg 1 Kings 21, Micah 2.1-10, Zechariah 7.9-14). The people of God must to repent and turn back to the Lord.

Often the people of Israel did not listen. Indeed God sometimes said that they would not listen (eg Isaiah 6.8-10, Ezekiel 3.4-11). But the prophets also spoke of the 'remnant of Israel' (eg Jeremiah 23.1-4, Amos 9.8-12, Zephaniah 3.11-13), chosen by God from 'lowly and poor people' whose poverty of spirit would enable them to hear 'the words of God' and repent. Then God would renew the covenant with the people of Israel (eg Jeremiah 32.37-41, Zephaniah 3.14-20, Zechariah 8.1-17). Some pictures of Israel's restoration verge on the fantastical, but the essence of them is that people have good reason to rejoice when they experience the grace of forgiveness and renewed friendship with God.

We are no more willing than the people of Israel to hear the message of prophecy. The truth is often unwelcome, forcing us to admit we are not all we pretend to ourselves or to others. We are angry if we are told that our image of God has fossilised into an idol; that our worship is empty because it does not affect the way we treat others; that the good cause to which we have given so much energy is less worthy than we thought and may even have harmed others. We do not wish to limit our freedoms for the benefit of weaker members in our society: we like to think our bit of charity work is enough. We aren't like those condemned by the prophets, are we? Surely God must see that. But no, ultimately God demands our all, asking us to see others through God's loving eyes. So God brings us to the *krisis* whose acceptance opens the door to the saving grace that enables us to use our suffering for spiritual growth and to find creative solutions for serious problems.

The first Hebrew prophet was Moses who led the Israelites into the wilderness: in that place of testing (Exodus 15.25b-26) they were often found wanting. Because they did not listen or wait for the word of the Lord they were tempted into idolatry, shirking the hard ethical work which would make them into a strong faith community, failing to use the hardship to strengthen them for the challenges ahead, and belly-aching: 'why did we ever come out of Egypt?' (Numbers 11.20). Elijah heard God speaking to him in the wilderness, and other prophets pointed to the people's learning experience in the wilderness (eg Jeremiah 2.2-7, Ezekiel 20.10-20). In the wilderness John the Baptist, the last Hebrew prophet, preached repentance (Matthew 3.1-12, Mark 1.1-8, Luke 3.1-20). Fittingly the temptations of Jesus were set in the wilderness (eg

Matthew 3.1-12) and Jesus sometimes went there to pray (Luke 5.16). So good precedents exist for using the wilderness experience to commune with God and search the depths of our being.

Depression is a wilderness experience, a judgement on the way of life which caused or exacerbated our illness, a *krisis* which offers the possibility of new life. Not all who stand on the edge of the Church have suffered depression - though I am surprised at the number who have - but most recognise the wilderness as a familiar experience on our spiritual journey. God may be calling us to invite the people of God in the Church to join us in the wilderness, where things may look very different away from the security of the institution; where we are thrown on the resources of God; where we have to listen for the murmurings of wisdom which rise from the ground of our being; where we have to live by faith and to travel hopefully; where we begin to see ourselves in the light of God's love, to find out who we really are and who we are meant to be; where we may discover what are our priorities, for it is only then that we can begin to help others to find theirs. God calls us into the wilderness and calls us back at intervals, to renew the covenant: 'I shall be your God and you shall be my people...' And the way to the promised land lies through the wilderness.

If we ask the people of God to join us in the wilderness, some, perhaps many, will refuse and may see those who journey into the wilderness as threats to the Church. We may be treated like the servants in the parable of the wicked vine-growers (eg Mark 12.1-12). Perhaps those who embark on that journey must be prepared to be the suffering servants of the Church or even to be the remnant of the people of God. I say this with great hesitation, in fear and trembling even, for we are not Hebrew prophets thundering 'this is the word of the Lord': we are called into the wilderness to hear what God may be saying to us as individuals and as the people of God. Those who have been in the wilderness for some time may have formulated some tentative questions to discuss with those who may join us. Such questions will be influenced by the 'on the edge' experience, but they may be the more valid for that. I have phrased them in the first person plural: if some of them are God's questions they are intended for all of us.

Is the loving will of God - what we know with the whole of our being is good for us and for others - the centre of all that we do? Do we recognise when our actions belie our words and when the various parts of our personality are in conflict? Do we follow Jesus in seeing God in everyone, in believers of other faiths as much as in Christians, in those of little faith as much as in those of firm faith, in enemies as much as in friends, in the poor as much as in the rich? Do we trust God's love to transform others into what God would have them be, so that we become less eager to change them into what we think they should be, so that we listen to their real concerns rather than answer the questions we think they should ask? Are we confident in God's love for us, so that we can admit that we do not have all the answers, so that we wrestle with the complexity and uncertainty of what love may demand of us rather than seek refuge in the safety of rules that may make us self-righteous, unforgiving and unloving? Knowing our own need of forgiveness, do we strive to forgive others? Recognising our inability to love, do we open ourselves to God's grace which has the power to renew our love?

Knowing that beliefs may fossilise and die, dare we define our beliefs less rigidly, so that each of us may find our own truth? Do we believe that authority resides in the truth alone when individuals and communities come to know what is true for them, so that we may lay down our 'top-down' and 'power-over' models of authority and liberate the creativity of the whole people of God? Can we worry less about unity or uniformity of belief than about giving priority to the love of God which binds Christians together? Can we be truthful about where we are on our journey rather than feel we must assent to beliefs that are not yet accepted by the fullness of our personality? Can we be honest when we disagree with this or remain agnostic about that part of the Church's traditional teaching, so that we encourage honesty in others? Can we be more adventurous in expressing our faith in the language and thought forms of each new generation, giving up some things hallowed by years of tradition so that our worship may come alive to those who seek the ministry of the Church, especially at birth, marriage and death? Dare we surrender the security that our church may offer against the realities of life, so that we may embrace life in all its fullness?

Can we see the plurality of beliefs as a rich source for the free spiritual and moral growth of individuals and communities? Do we share what we believe in a spirit of love and humility, confessing that Christian evangelism may have given a message of moral superiority and may have damaged the tolerance that our pluralist society needs to thrive? Can we be committed to our Christian faith and also accept that other faiths offer believers a saving knowledge of the God of many names? Can we express our Christian faith in words, images and actions that do not require hearers to share the Hebrew and Greek world view out from which Christianity grew? Can we give up our claims to absolute truth, without selling the pass to other religious faiths who make similar claims, so that we reduce conflict with other faiths and within the Christian Church? Can we work in loving cooperation with all who embrace spiritual values?

What other questions might God be asking? We shall not know unless we listen, and listening is perhaps the most important element in worship.

CHAPTER 15

REVIVING WORSHIP

With slick words
and catchy tunes
you really did them proud
They swayed to the music
of your adman Christianity
With arms upraised
they closed their dreamy eyes
feeling uplifted
strengthened
renewed
for the Jesus March

But it won't do

We don't live in Bible times
We are not a first century audience
satisfied
with less than scientific proof
We do not accept things
on authority

because the Bible says
what it says
is all and always true
And to say
it more loudly
more brightly
more cleverly
may impress for a while
but does not make it true

No, it won't do

This protest was occasioned by the uncritical use of biblical language in a televised service. Many churches use liturgies based on the Bible or on the worship of the early Church. Too often those liturgies find modern equivalents for ancient words without modernising the concepts of a pre-scientific and patriarchal age: the supernatural metaphysics and the male patriarchy of Bible times remain but without the cloak of mystery and ambiguity provided by the old language. The job of modernisation seems only half done, and if worship is to come alive in each generation, we need new words, images and concepts that do not commit us to supernatural and hierarchical views of reality, that prompt us to move beyond traditional male images of God to metaphors that reveal more of the mystery. Many will refuse to give up familiar and reassuring words, insisting that they alone are validated by the Bible or by tradition, but only the hard creative work of re-imaging God will put us on the leading edge of discovery and revitalise our worship.

Feeling that I would enjoy putting my mind to this problem I began work on a book about worship in schools - 'interesting, but it won't sell 5000 copies' - and I looked for places where worship was alive and challenging. I was delighted to find one or two, but while I was depressed I found it hard to worship:

In the warmth of the worship
I felt tense
almost to the point of rushing out
I strangled the rising panic
without naming its source
Was it alienation I felt?
Alienation from what or from whom?
Most members
anxious to elicit the views of others
spoke softly
even tentatively
of the truth they had discovered
and few strident voices jarred
not enough to make me feel apart
Was my alienation
the loneliness of doubt
amid apparent certainty?
Or was I alienated
from the what or whom of God
that I still cannot feel?

I came to see my doubt as healthy, as a path to faith and a defence against idolatry (see chapter 3), but I was less sure about my sense of alienation from God, though I knew depressed people often feel it. I turned to the Psalms. Although we may want to read them with caveats because our image of God has changed, the Psalms (and other biblical poetry such as Job, Proverbs, Song of Songs, Lamentations and parts of the Prophets) often express the raw emotions – anger, wonder, fear, depression, gratitude, vengeance, joy – that tumble out of people in crisis or in celebration. So we may use the poetry to voice our feelings or to explore what they may be. I read the Psalms through quickly, pausing only to mark those verses which seemed to strike a chord with my present mood and then I made a short poem from some of those verses:

Why have you forsaken me?
Why are you so far from saving me
so far from heeding my groans
By day I cry to you
but there is no answer
In the night I cry
with no respite
Tears are my food day and night
while all day long people ask me:
Where is your God?
You are my God
Why have you rejected me?

My sense of alienation turned out to be a feeling that God had abandoned me. Had God really left me? Would the God of love, who runs to meet the repenting child and goes out to seek and save the lost, forsake me at the point when I was repenting, recognising my collusion in the twisted games of our sad family? Psychotherapy made me aware that a much more primitive image of God still lurked in my unconscious, an angry God who was out to get me. Somehow I must rid myself of such a false image, tear down the idol I had made (see chapter 5), discover the real God through Jesus (chapter 11) and find salvation (chapter 12). The sequence of these chapters suggests a step by step process, but it was not like that. Often I seemed to be drifting powerless in the uncharted waters of my unconscious, lost in the fog out of which icebergs loomed too late to avoid a collision. My mind lacked power to get me under way, charts to show me where to go or light to penetrate the fog. I needed to engage more of my faculties in the process of re-imaging the God of my unconscious. Might worship enable me to bring more of myself to my quest for the real God? How could worship do that when I still felt so uncomfortable with it?

Then the sculpture I mentioned in chapter 14 gave me hope that worship might pilot me through the uncharted foggy waters. This is how I tried to tell Jessica what her gift meant to me:

What is it that I have been given?
I am entranced
by the reflection of creation
in the careful shaping of body and limb
the intricate weaving of colour
and the conveying of emotion
I feel and know
the sadness of the dark figure
hiding
and half-hidden by the vine
which glows in the dark
and which conceals
but does not imprison
the bird of heaven
in the bole of the tree
I am gladdened
by the mother
who wants her son
to venture on his own
yet proffers a hand
to encourage and to catch
lest he fall
Will he dare to walk alone?
I share her delight
in the flowers
that he brings to her
The whole speaks to me

of the possibility
of new life
amid the sadness of the old
of the opportunity
to complete the good work
the work
of prophecy
for which I was created

What is it that I have been given?
I am overwhelmingly conscious
of the labour of love and prayer
which this gift represents
I feel uplifted and loved
I am more grateful
than words can say
I hug you, Jessica

The sculpture became an unspoken prayer, a way to open myself to the mystery of God. I would focus my eyes on it as I tried to still my unquiet mind by bringing my breathing under control and saying to myself 'love' on the inbreath and 'peace' on the out. If that did not work, I used a mantra. When distressed I would repeat 'Underneath are the everlasting arms' (Deuteronomy 33.27 - AV); when anxious, 'Let be then; learn that I am God' (Psalm 46.10); when feeling unloved, 'God's love endures for ever' (adapted from Psalm 136). Used in this way the sculpture seemed to resonate with something deep within, putting me in touch, however tenuously, with the real God.

I was helped too by reflecting on something I had heard Edward Patey say years before: 'worship is truth and love as we explore them.' This sentence now caught fire, liberating me from my old view of worship - ascribing worth to God - and offering me a new vision. Worship is for all who see that their truth is only part of a greater whole and their love less than ideal, whether they use God language or not. Worship means being honest with ourselves so that we may come to terms with who we are and who we might be in relation to others and to the truth and love that are greater than ourselves. Religious people may find the highest truth and love within the divine but all may come to live more at ease with the mystery at the heart of life by exploring truth in the light of love and love in the light of truth.

Seen this way worship was not something I was doing for God. God did not need my praise, at least not in the language of propitiation and adulation which seemed empty and better suited to an age when people thought of God as controlling the forces of nature, as holding their fate in his hands. The wonder of creation and the darkness of terror still spoke to me of the otherness of God, but I felt a need to explore the mysterious immanence of God, whose love might make me secure enough to grow from childhood dependence into 'the full stature of Christ' (Ephesians 4.13). So I began to explore ways of being with God - alone or with others - so that together we might honestly explore the mysterious givenness of life and love, of good and evil, of suffering and death.

While I was seriously depressed I became - to my surprise – much more appreciative of creation: I would stop to look at the sunset or to admire a baby. I sensed the ultimate mystery in the beauty of the sunset and the miracle of birth. Science may explain the processes which bring them to be but not their purpose. Our understanding of the mechanics of reproduction in no way lessens the miracle of new birth: a new life comes about through us, we feel the awe of creation and in the depths of our being we know that our baby is a gift to be treasured and nurtured, to be allowed to grow and go free. All we can do is to enjoy the gift – with full and grateful hearts. A joyous and thankful acceptance of the gift of life and all it brings enables us to live generously and creatively: seeing what is given as a right makes us so protective of what is ours that we lose our spontaneity and love.

Exploring the mystery of creation in wonder and thankfulness led me to two truths: that we are tiny parts of a universe whose vastness we cannot grasp, grains in the sands of time - a lesson in true humility; and that, however small we may be, we are unique and so infinitely valuable. Many passages in the Bible (eg Psalm 8) recognise this and Jesus spoke of God's concern for each and every person (eg Matthew 10.29-31). Science also points to the unique genetic make-up of each human being. So both theology and science give us cause to celebrate the value of this one-off creation, this you and this me.

Reaching an intellectual conclusion and feeling its truth are not the same thing. While I knew that God loved me the distorted thinking of my depressed brain stopped me feeling loved. Often sacraments intended to celebrate God's love seemed so hedged around with provisos ('if you repent.., if you believe...') that I felt more judged than loved in church. That made me angry, for the sculpture, my meditation on the parable of the prodigal son (see chapter 12) and the love of those who cared for me when I was at my worst suggested to some deep part of me that I might risk putting my trust in God's love. Tentatively, with the aid of another sculpture, I imagined myself held in love while I faced the real me and explored what love might make of me. My anger kept me away from church - for a long time I could worship with others only in silence or in less formal settings - but it helped me to purge my unconscious of some primitive images of God, though at times they return in other forms to haunt me and I have to go through the process again. Slowly I learned more of the negative emotions hidden in the shadow side of my unconscious, naming them, accepting them as my own, recognising how I had denied or projected them, confessing them. I was warned not to 'bewail my manifest sins and wickedness,' not to be too hard on myself (I am not responsible for the feelings that arise in me, but only for what I do with them). So I tried to proceed with love, gentleness and humour, but also to persist, for coming to know myself was, and is, a slow process, hindered by two obstacles.

The first was fear, the nameless dread which often afflicts the depressed. As I became more sure that I was loved, I found the courage to face my fear and so began to understand how it originated in the events of my childhood and how from its hiding place in my shadow it had fed my anxiety for years. Love exposed my fear for the fraud it was and I was surprised at how much energy was released, energy I had wasted in keeping it locked away. My fear diminished only slowly and fitfully, but the courage that came from love did wonders for my self-respect and as it receded I felt freer, fuller and more able to love.

The second obstacle was the guilt which had paralysed me, preventing me from acting even to rid myself of the guilt. As I became more convinced that I was loved, I saw that I was using guilt to punish myself for falling short of the unrealistic standards I had imbibed in childhood. I must decide for myself what standards I judged it right to live by, bring my childhood conditioning to trial against those standards, and learn to forgive myself as I was forgiven by God and others who loved me. It was, and is, a hard struggle, made more difficult by the Church's long-held belief that original sin makes human beings incapable of being good. Self-righteousness may prevent us from seeing our faults and good may be perverted by evil, but to function well as human beings we need confidence, confidence in ourselves that we can make progress, confidence from others that they trust us. Balanced and integrated people are aware of their shadow but set it in the context of their good qualities and hard-won achievements.

Confession needs to come from the heart (eg Joel 2.12-13) but it is hard to hear what our heart is saying amid the noise generated by our busy conscious ego. We need to listen for the 'faint murmuring sound' which arises from our unconscious and which may be the voice of God (1 Kings 19). When we pray we need to talk less and listen more. Perhaps that is why I found that silence helped me most. Many fear silence and fill it with words and music but I have found that silence, alone or with others, can gather an intensity which speaks more loudly than words, enabling me to be with my whole self and to explore its depths, allowing images to form and rise to consciousness, bringing love, forgiveness, healing and peace. Such a silence calls me to repent, to turn away from the pretence that has been towards the true self that God wants me to be.

Because we are all in varying degrees proud, angry, jealous, lustful, gluttonous, avaricious and lazy, we are wise to admit our failings. If I pretend to be better than I am some people may be convinced for some of the time and I may be convinced in some parts of my being, but the pretence may make me self-righteous, so that I deny my faults but make few allowances for others, or project them onto others, blaming them for what is mine. Pretence is the stuff that pharisees are made of, and pharisees cannot love and be loved, cannot love themselves, because they live in fear that their pretence will be exposed (1 John 4.18). The silence enabled me to be honest about myself, to face the *krisis* which showed me how my fear of anger caused me to deny being angry, to the cost of my health and the well-being of those around me; how close my touchiness in defending myself against accusation was to the self-righteousness I condemned in others; how my shadow had undermined my relationships with others. The *krisis* was cleansing, helping me to end the loneliness of pretence, to learn the truth about myself and to open myself to the love and forgiveness of God.

Of course there is much hidden in my shadow that still needs to be brought into the light of God's love and forgiveness, as my dreams show:

The drains are blocked again
not quite to overflowing
The septic tank is quite dried out
offering nourishing humus to the garden
Perhaps I should dig it out and spread it
before I tackle the blockage

The drain is too long for the rods
however much I try to extend them
by makeshift arrangements
I must look for another manhole
Under layer upon layer
of carpet and flooring
I find it
The rods reach the blockage
but I awake
before the sewage flows

So my confession and my *krisis* continue, but I no longer feel judged or threatened by the false images of God which lurk in the recesses of my unconscious or which others may preach at me. Whatever remains to be confessed, I know that I am loved.

My need of forgiveness challenges me to forgive the faults and failings of others. That is not easy. Some of the hurts of my childhood were so searing that I buried them: I could not forgive them because it was too painful even to admit their existence. Some betrayals and deceits in my professional life caused me to boil with fury or seethe with vengeful thoughts, but often I could not say how I really felt: my bottled up feelings prevented me from forgiving the hurts that caused them. When psychotherapy put me in touch with my feelings, I began with trepidation to express some of them in drawing, painting and writing. And the writing became a sort of worship. On a Sunday morning I would begin with a time of silent reflection from which grew the free verse in this book and much more. Gradually I came to terms with my wounds and began the process of forgiving. I sometimes had to forgive the same offence over and over again as I came to appreciate how hurt I had been or as events reopened the wound from time to time (Matthew 18.21-22).

I also had to learn to forgive with the whole of my being. It was easy to say 'I forgive you' with the rational mind because that wins approval, but I often harboured contrary feelings in my unconscious. I sometimes discovered what these were by meditating on the stories of the Bible. When I read the stories as stories without trying to find a moral or believing that they took place exactly as written, I found a new richness of meaning. I focussed on stories that appealed to me, trying to forget the interpretations laid on them. I would ask myself what images and symbols affected me strongly; which characters appealed to me and which did not; which inspired my love and trust or my fear and anger; with which - being as honest as I could be - I really identified. In this way I came to see myself as the elder brother in the parable of the prodigal son, and that was a real turning point.

As I worked in this way the early myths of Genesis struck a chord with something deep within and offered me choices: I could accept the gift of life or turn my back upon it; I could work with God to find my true self and maximise my potential for love or turn my back on God and deny life and love. The myth of the exodus from Egypt, the wanderings in the wilderness and the entry to the promised land became my spiritual journey, celebrated in a rewriting of Psalm 136:

It is good to give thanks to God
whose love endures for ever

For the mysterious gifts
of life and of love
I thank God
whose love endures for ever
For the darkness of depression
which is the darkness of God
I thank God
whose love endures for ever
For deliverance from the witches

and the puritan
I thank God
whose love endures for ever
For tearing down the idols
and ridding me of false images
I thank God
whose love endures for ever
For the krisis
which reveals me as I am
I thank God
whose love endures for ever
For the forgiving love
which accepts me as I am
I thank God
whose love endures for ever
For the wilderness vision
which encourages me to become
who God would have me be
I thank God
whose love endures for ever
For the mysterious givenness
of evil suffering and death
I thank God
whose love endures for ever
For the saving grace
which offers new possibility
amid sorrow and despair
I thank God
whose love endures for ever
For the wounds of life
which open me to the needs of others
I thank God

whose love endures for ever
For the journey towards the promised land
wherever and whatever that may be
I thank God
whose love endures for ever

It is good to give thanks to God
whose love endures for ever

I rejoiced too in the stories of Jesus. Because Jesus left us to draw our own conclusions (except when the Gospel writer felt he must add an explanation), a parable may not evoke a response in us straightaway. However reflecting upon a parable and imagining myself in each of the roles makes it come alive for me when I need it. The same approach bears fruit with the healing miracles and other incidents in the life of Jesus. I was offered healing when in meditation I pictured my pain, fear and rage entering the pigs like Legion's unclean spirits and being carried away over the cliff (Mark 5.1-20), and I learned much about my attitudes to women and to people of different races and religions by being imaginatively present at the well of Sychar (John 4.4-30).

So stories, particularly Bible stories, may teach us wisdom, enabling us to explore what we think and feel, to find purpose and meaning in life, to confront the realities of evil, suffering and death, to know our potential for evil and for good, to weigh the effect of our actions, to decide by what values to live, to gain confidence and courage, to release our creativity and imagination, to embrace change, or to find forgiveness, healing and love. Stories linger in the mind when we have forgotten the sermon and as we ponder them they may bring us inspiration and insight when we most need it.

It is perhaps natural in depression to focus on ourselves but while I was seriously depressed I was challenged by the terminal illness of Danny:

Perhaps I should not wonder
that I am in turmoil
in the milieu of the hospital
or of the sick room
haunted by the ghosts
of past trauma
which not even the loving kindness
that I now encounter
can exorcise
It is hard to be loving
amid echoes and ghosts

Confessing the poverty of my heart and my inability to carry on loving opened the way for the gift of grace that renewed my love and enabled me to cope. I took strength from the central story of the Gospels, the myth of the death and resurrection of Jesus, which seemed to say that God would bring new life even out of the tragic death of a young child. As Danny was dying we saw new life in my elderly mother who learned from him how to shrug off the aches and pains of age and how to find rich enjoyment in a life limited by growing infirmity. We are now seeing new life in the contribution Danny's mother is making out of the wounds she received in Danny's short life. Danny taught me that loving means being vulnerable, using our wounds in the service of others, risking that our weakness may be exploited or our wounds reopened. We dare take that risk only when we are ourselves strengthened by the love of others and by the love of God, when we know that love will heal reopened wounds.

Prayer could not undo the damage wrought in Danny's lungs by cystic fibrosis but it did enable the power of God, love-in-the-form-of-grace, to bring hope out of despair, joy out of sorrow, and new life after death. Ours were the hearts and hands through which God showed love to the sorrowing and so prayer was not about changing the external circumstances - much though we wished it would - but about changing us, altering our inward state, changing how we saw things and how we related to them, putting us in touch with the depths of our being and renewing our love, so that love could bring what healing and wholeness was possible within the natural law. Through prayer we began to set Danny's suffering and the suffering of those around him in the perspective of love, so that we could live with the mysterious givenness of it and find God within it (see chapter 13).

Danny's death, my family's sad history and my depressive illness left me so vulnerable that the news or some other affecting scene on the television would make me cry. Perhaps crying is a proper response to the world's pain when there seems little else we can do, but normally we switch off literally or metaphorically - because we cannot cope with so much tragedy. Prayer is an antidote to switching-off for it helps us to see others through the eyes of God as uniquely valuable, to strengthen our resolve to fight for the justice which is the outworking of love in the world, and to work out the proper balance between loving our neighbours and loving ourselves. The distortions that depression caused in my thinking meant that such prayer was beyond me and so for a long time I avoided the news or reduced its impact by listening to a midday bulletin on the radio. The only prayer I managed when overwhelmed by the needs of others was 'Let be then, let God.' As my recovery has progressed I have begun to identify the areas where I can serve: some are new ways of using my training and experience but others have grown out of my wounds. And I am more able to say no: I know that I am not called to do more than I am able (1 Corinthians 10.13) and that it lies between God and me to decide where to draw the line.

For that reason I still have to be wary of the shoulds, oughts and musts from my past and of new ones that people may try to impose on me. That may be one reason why I found sermons difficult, particularly when powerful preachers played on my emotions. I thought that there must be a better way of arriving at what is true for me than listening to a preacher 'six feet above contradiction.' What might I learn from the experiences of all the worshippers? Might we replace the sermon with a dialogue in which no one tried to impose a particular view but everyone sought to share what they had found true for themselves? If each worshipper awaited the promptings of the spirit before speaking, and if what was spoken was received in silence so that it could be pondered in the heart before the mind was distracted by the next contribution, might we have a means of sharing many differing and even contradictory apprehensions of truth?

I have found such dialogue in the worship of Kaleidoscope, the Movement for the Ordination of Women and the Religious Society of Friends, but it is inhibited where liturgy, ritual, vestments and seating signal the importance of the preacher or celebrant, implying that worship is something he or she does to us or for us. Many churches cannot be easily rearranged to enable people to talk to each other, dance, perform, make music, paint, draw or write. But we need these languages, if we are to find the creativity that involves our whole being, our senses, our emotions and our intellect. Worship should stir us, making us laugh and cry. It should shake us, disturbing our complacency, changing us, setting us on fire. It should encourage us to express, however imperfectly or tentatively, what is just beyond our comprehension, at the leading edge of discovery. When all our faculties are actively involved in the dialogue enacted in the presence of God our truth may be enlarged in the perspective of God's love for us and our fellow human beings. And we are more likely to be honest about what we feel and think, so that God's grace may renew and expand our love.

I came to live more at ease with myself and what needs to be done in the world when I understood that love was less a duty and more a joy. If we love with joy in our hearts, we shall share the wealth of creation, being neither niggardly nor spendthrift, not making a virtue out of abstinence. Joy has a way of reducing suffering, enabling us to put our own suffering and that of others into perspective, releasing energy for our healing and theirs. Joy causes us to celebrate and there is so much to celebrate in worship: our wonder at the universe; our thankfulness for the gift of life; our common humanity and the interdependence which asks us to work together; our successes in personal or communal tasks; the values and beliefs that we share; the grace of salvation and our journey to spiritual health and wholeness; the memory of significant stages in personal and communal life; the myths which express our deepest understanding of the nature of our being and our life on earth; the love in creation that surrounds new birth; the parental love that stands back as the child grows to adulthood; the love in partnership which creates a marriage; the love-in-the-form-of-grace which comes when we face suffering; the love remembered after the death of a loved one.

Much that we celebrate in worship is common to the human race. We might even replace the word 'God' with 'love' in this chapter and there would still be much left that we could see as worship, exploring truth and love, finding ways of apprehending the mystery within and about us, promoting the personal growth and psychological wholeness of individuals, fostering loving relationships between people. The value of worship does not depend on its language or form, for the spirit of truth and love flies free while words and forms may ossify. The value of worship rests on the extent to which it brings the harvest of the spirit: love, joy, peace, patience, kindness, goodness, fidelity, gentleness and self-control (Galatians 5.22-23).

CHAPTER 16

BECOMING MYSELF

Recovery from depressive illness is a slow process. Anti-depressants do not effect a cure: they prop up our battered metabolism while our body replaces the neuro-transmitters destroyed by our over-use of stress hormones. Recovery comes when we have enough neuro-transmitters to make safe and secure connections between the nerves of the central nervous system. However during our recovery we cannot entirely avoid using the accelerator - all kinds of events put us under stress - and so we may further damage our neuro-transmitters. Thus the progress of recovery is rarely smooth, more like three steps forward and two back. Reverses can seem devastating, especially when the medication is increased to levels greater than ever before, perhaps because the liver has found a way of breaking down the drug. We should try to judge our progress from how we felt at the lowest point of the depression, not how we felt yesterday.

I found this hard to learn. When I felt better I saw no reason why I should not do more. I thought that once the level of medication was reduced I would be able to go on as before. I would find another job, less stressful than before, and get on with my life. Each time we took advantage of springtime to reduce the medication, something happened to blow my recovery off course, perhaps something serious such as the attempted suicide of a friend or the illness of my mother, maybe something seemingly trivial such as an invitation back to the college or a meeting at church. Even small events might make demands on my emotional energy, because they were invested with more emotional significance than I at first perceived and so depleted my neuro-transmitters. At one stage we kept a book to record such debits so that I would take the necessary rest and relaxation before exerting myself once more. It was hard to live within myself, to listen to the cycles of exhaustion and energy and to remember that exhaustion might bring the black mood back.

Like many in our society I had a hang-up about work. In recent years government and society have so reinforced the old Protestant work ethic that we value work as next to godliness, measuring people's worth by the job they do and their status by how much they earn. The creation of wealth has become the nation's priority, no doubt so that good things may follow, but in practice wealth seems more important than the greatest happiness of the greatest number, the development of personal qualities, and the ideals of service to the community and to those less fortunate than ourselves. To be unemployed is to be stigmatised as idle or scrounging; to be a housewife, a carer or a pensioner is to be deprived of status; to be poor is to be of no account; to be off work through depression or some other stress-induced illness is to be despised as weak. Too harsh a judgement, some may cry, but many TV adverts give the message that happiness is what money can buy, and when politicians talk of incentives do they ever mean anything other than money?

Could I stop my collusion with what I now see is a lie? Even though I now know that I am loved for what I am and not for what I can do (see chapter 12), for many years I behaved as if my value did depend on what I achieved at work, as if I could buy status and security by working harder, without counting the cost in terms of the health and happiness of myself and others. I was proud of my hard work and the praise of others tempted me to say yes when I should have said no. Why was I so blind?

As a child I often heard my father say 'if at first you don't succeed, try, try and try again.' I am sure his intention was to ensure that I should take the opportunities that he had never had, not that I should make up for his failure to achieve the success he thought his abilities warranted. His dictum may have been appropriate at times but the child in me unwisely adopted it as a rule of life. Recognising this driving force in psychotherapy reduced its power without entirely eliminating it. I still have to fight my perfectionism: I know it is illogical, for no one is perfect and what I do has only to be good enough for its purpose. Yet I still become anxious when I do not reach the highest standards, sometimes so anxious that I cannot embark on a task for fear of failure. So I have to ask myself again: who says I must have such high standards and what more reasonable standards shall I choose for myself?

Roger Burford, the GP who first diagnosed my depressive illness, christened me the medallion man, saying that I had taken on the role of the knight in shining armour who would solve or carry the burden of the family's ills. I cared too much, felt too responsible for what happened, and accepted the double standard of caring for others while being critical of myself. And this spread to my work and many other aspects of my life. Again psychotherapy helped me to explain how my over-developed sense of responsibility had arisen, but it can still catch me unawares. So again I have to ask myself: who says I should or must be responsible for what other people do? I may be able to influence them for good but I cannot control them: they are responsible for their own actions.

At a time when I thought I might soon return to work, I set down some signposts to help me avoid the traps of perfectionism and over-responsibility and to point me to a more healthy lifestyle. The you I addressed is of course me!

1. KNOW WHY YOU ARE WORKING

You may think you know, but do you? Are you still trying to earn approval or love? Your value as a person does not rest on what you achieve. Is work an escape from other problems? It is better to face them. Are you trying to bury your depression? You may succeed for a while but not for long. Searching out the real reasons will expose them to your rational critique and enable you to set sensible objectives for your working life and to fulfil them without overstressing yourself.

2. PUT WORK INTO A PROPER PERSPECTIVE OF TIME AND ENERGY

Your time and energy belong to God, to you, your family and friends. Your employer buys a part of your week. Recreation, relaxation and sleep are vital to your health and effective working. So discipline your mind to switch off from work and onto family, friends and fun, perhaps picturing the solution of the current problem or using techniques of relaxation.

3. LISTEN TO YOUR BODY

Your body has its own wisdom. Accept its rhythms and cycles, being thankful when energy flows, and reining yourself back without guilt when it doesn't. Use breathing exercises until it becomes second nature to breathe through your tummy and not your chest. Find short but frequent times of quiet to relax consciously and if tension persists use relaxation exercises. Take exercise to flush away stress hormones.

4. PLAN YOUR WORK TIME

Establish the priority of tasks: estimate how long each will take assign the time and try to stick to it, even if you leave something unfinished. Leave time for the unexpected, for catching up and for proper breaks.

Planning your time gets more done and stops you worrying about which task you are going to do when.

5. KNOW YOUR LIMITS AND LIMITATIONS

When unreasonable demands are made of your time and energy or when a task is beyond your skill, it is better to say no at the start than to confess later that you haven't had time or to suffer the stress of over-commitment. Withstand the temptation to say yes to win approval. And resist blackmail, for blackmailers come back for more.

6. SHARE RESPONSIBILITY

If you cling to responsibility it becomes an ever-increasing burden: shared or delegated, it becomes lighter and more rewarding, but when you delegate, trust that the job will be done properly and on time, and stop fussing! When things go wrong, admit your mistakes and try to put them right (hiding them makes you defensive, irritates others and wastes emotional energy), but accept only your just share of the blame: gently but firmly point out the responsibility of others and the contribution of causes beyond your control.

7. THINK AND TALK POSITIVELY

Assume the best of people, including yourself, until proved wrong. Avoid the prophets of doom who may talk you into a depressive mood. Fight anxiety, for imagination creates many problems: concentrate on the real problems of today rather than the hypothetical ones of tomorrow. If something is worth doing, do not be inhibited by a fear of failure. Try not to be upset by criticism: it says nothing about your worth as a person and it may be helpful; if not, you can reject it, for only you know whether it is justified.

8. FIND OUTLETS FOR YOUR ANGER AND FRUSTRATION

It is all right to be angry. If you can, express it to the person who caused it, or if you can't, to a third party who will respect it. Unexpressed it may undermine your work and your health; stored up it may burst out when you least want it to; projected it may destroy your relationships. Is your anger caused by your unrealistic expectations of yourself or of others? Anger may be released by vigorous exercise or by letters to distant sources of frustration.

9. KEEP THE PAST OUT OF THE PRESENT

A counsel of perfection, for your past has made you what you are. But recognise when events echo happenings in the past and awaken childhood emotions, so that you may take steps to defuse the excess emotion. And if today is a bad day, do not carry it into tomorrow: make a fresh start each day.

10. REMEMBER THAT PERSONAL GROWTH IS SLOW BUT SURE

Falls and upsets are par for the course: they do not signify failure but give you the chance to learn by your mistakes and to recognise the progress that you have made towards a more healthy life.

Although I have not yet returned to employment, these signposts have been very helpful, not least in enabling me to put my previous work life into a proper perspective. However they seem to assume recovery to something like I was before. But that is not the case, for two reasons: I have wounds to carry and I am not the same person.

We have seen how I have been wounded by the events of my childhood and by the blows that life has dealt me. My childhood wounds caused me to make such maladaptions to life that I was less well-equipped than I might have been to handle pressures and difficulties. Psychotherapy has helped me to understand the wounds of childhood, to bandage some and heal others, but I am hampered by bandages and scars. I cannot go back to a might-have-been childhood and start again. Likewise the wounds of later life have left me with scars or bandages and I must do the best I can within the limitations they impose.

I cannot go entirely free
I shall carry
the wounds inflicted in my youth
when I believed
in the dragon and the witches
when I was burned
by the real fire of my imagination
But the dragon is dead
and I climb the scales of his neck
as a stairway
leaving the witches as shadows
in the crypt below
and the fire under control

Standing on the floor of the church
I push open the door
peering into the light
of the sun-drenched meadow
It takes time for my eyes
to adjust to the brightness
before I can see
the road winding
towards the deep blue river

I step outside
aware at once of sunflowers
growing from graves in the churchyard
Shall I pick them for a posy
or leave them to reflect
the sun in their differing hues?
I pass them by
as I set out
towards the waiting punt

It is tempting
to take short cuts across the grass
but all the short cuts lead
back to the beginning
and I find myself back in the church
or worse
back in the crypt
struggling
with the dragon and the witches
Unwillingly
I learn it is quicker
to follow the winding road

As I journey towards the sun
the road winds to the east
and I become aware of a bright darkness
As it winds to the west
I travel beneath a pale sky
Reaching the river
I choose to punt upstream
against the slow-moving water
I punt gently towards the source

resting a while in the island
as the moon gleams from a darkening sky

Even at the relatively early stage that I wrote this (soon after the second of the pictures mentioned in chapter 1) I had begun to view my wounds more positively. I could see a brighter future. I did not know then how disabling my wounds might be: I had to wait - and I am still waiting - to know when I shall be able to return to some form of employment. At a later stage I realised what my wounds might teach me:

I have wounds to carry
which limit what I can do
They remind me
that I am vulnerable
that I must tread warily around witches
for they have the power
to plunge me back into the black hole
that I must shun the puritan preacher
who has the power
to rekindle the fires of self-destruction
that pushing myself to the limit
carries the risk of further injury
that new ventures require a secure base
that 'I enjoy' is a better motive
than 'I ought'
that I can say no

If I listen to what my wounds are trying to say to me, I can learn much from them, and I can share that learning with other people. I sometimes find it hard to know when to speak of them - I do not want to force my experience on others when it may not be appropriate to their circumstances - but sometimes when I feel constrained to tell how it was for me others seem able to tell some of their own story in a way that brings relief or healing. I try not to give advice, for people must find their own solutions, but after one sharing of painful experience with friends of ours I was moved to offer this:

Judith, I hear your pain
feel your anguish
understand how you are driven
to a desert place
Resist the siren voices
who tempt you
to be other than you are
Stay true to the inner voice
telling you to journey
in the wilderness
towards your promised land
Remember
there is manna in the wilderness
and a pillar of cloud or of fire
to lead you on your way

Living without assurance
do not go
where assurance is acclaimed
with such vigour
that it is not real
where it rings
hollow in an empty shell

Living on the edge
look for soft edges
with hard centres

for hard edges increase your pain
and soft centres offer no hope

Living in doubt
worship only
where believers know
they are uncertain of their ground
for only in doubt
can you find faith

Living in pain
know that you cannot escape
Flight now brings more pain later
The only way forward
is through the pain
but in the journey
you will meet joy

Living in fear
know that you cannot flee
else fear will dog your days
If you look your fear in the face
you will find courage
you do not know you have
In that courage hope is born

Living in anger
accept it as your own
without guilt
You are not responsible
for the emotions that arise within
but only for what you do with them

Freed from guilt
you can begin to transform
the fire of anger
into the fire of love

Living in grief
allow yourself to mourn
Tears carry away the stress
of rage at the dying of the light
which once lit your path
and now is gone
Allow the tears to flow
and you will find within them
new love joy hope and peace

Judith, there is no easy way
to find who you are
and are meant to be
There is no universal truth
to give you all the answers
There is only the journey
towards your own truth
On the most difficult roads
there are cairns upon the way
and your travelling companions
who love you
will hold and support you
when the going is rough

This was a wisdom that spoke from the depths of depression, a wisdom that was not available to me before, and I became conscious that I had changed and was changing. I am still changing. I am learning to listen to deep parts of my being of which I was unaware before. I am more in touch with my shadow, more ready to acknowledge what lies there. I can admit that I am angry, because I feel less guilty and am less afraid of it, and so I waste less energy concealing it. I find that anger is useful in the way that pain may be: it is a warning bell telling me to take notice of what I feel. I am more able to express it and to use it creatively. And much the same is true of the other feelings I have named and faced. I am better at recognising the people I have internalised and at understanding the damage they did to the child within. I am willing to let that child speak and play more freely:

The abused child
could no longer remain imprisoned
She first
then he
demanded to be heard
loved and comforted
demanded to be healed
demanded to be allowed to grow
For that child to be heard
meant plunging into the depths of depression
going through the terror
of being unloved and hated
of not knowing the way
out of the morass onto solid ground
or out of the dark into light
It meant being willing
to feel the pain
to allow the dark feelings
to come upon me
to dare to defuse the timebomb of rage
It meant accepting

that the only way out of the pain
is through

It felt dangerous. I might lose my sanity or my life. I might lose my nerve, draw back from the edge and so lose the chance to know the unforeseen and creative opportunities that might exist outside my prison. I had to find the courage, the strength and the vision to break free. In the Roman arena a gladiator (in this case a *retiarius* armed only with a net) greets the Emperor of Rome in Latin: 'Hail, Caesar, we who are about to die salute you.'

Ave Caesar
morituri te salutamus

You wear the purple
and lord it over us still
after two thousand years
You claim absolute power
over heart and soul
choosing those who are sent
to face the lions
armed only with a net

The lions are caught
in the deceit of the trapper's net
caged
and brought from Africa
snarling
They are fed
enough to keep them alive
but not enough to satisfy
They are hungry
when they are released

one by one
into the arena
there to face the retiarius
armed with the net
that symbolises captivity

The lion is surprised by the noise
as you
and the common herd you hate
cheer on the retiarius
while you will the lion
to tear him to pieces

What has the retiarius done
to earn his fate?
He has refused to worship you
as a god
And so you give him
a web of lies
to ensnare the king of the beasts
a noble independent cat
at ease with himself
using his power
only to catch his prey
to feed himself and his pride
to defend his females and cubs

Moving with sensual grace
great strength under perfect control
the lion stalks his prey
cautious as he sees the net
As he leaps

he is distracted
for a split second
by the roar of the crowd
anticipating blood on the white sand
In that moment
the retiarius sways to one side
enveloping the lion in the net
Exhausted by his struggles
he is carried back to his cage
far beneath the podium of your throne
There he recovers his strength

He renews the battle
with one retiarius
then another
for other lions escape the net
to make a kill
delighting your perverted mind
and satisfying the blood lust
of the mob you despise
The lion learns
slowly
not to listen to the shrieking women
He waits patiently
and pounces
avoiding the net
to make his kill
Tearing meat from his prey
he watches as his warders encircle him
with more nets
for lions who have made one kill
are hungry for another

and the vulgar crowd pay more
His warders are skilled
and many against one
He cannot evade the nets
and is returned to his cage

Many times the lion returns to the arena
Many times he makes a kill
Many times he is recaptured
to fight another day
Many times he tries a new tactic
feinting this way and that
One lucky day
a warder is caught off guard
one blow of a powerful paw
one leap
and he is free
free in your Roman Capitol
a wild beast striking fear
into the populace you contemn
hunted but not caught by your army
Cats small and large move silently
and at night
Slinking through the shadows
down the Appian Way
the cat turns east
to the wildness of the Appennines

Not under African skies
he is more wary
but the ferocity of the arena fades
and he kills only to feed

He misses his African pride
but he lives graciously
among the other animals
who slowly recognise him
shadow that he is of his African self
as their king
If his sleep is sometimes restless
it is because he dreams
of the purple and the nets
If he seems smaller
he is a cat still
and he is free

As I was writing a line from an ode by Horace came into my mind: '*Odi profanum vulgus et arceo*' or 'I hate the unholy masses and I keep away from them.' I used it in the poem three times in various translations. When I had finished I looked up the ode and my eye was drawn to the next two lines: 'Hush your voices; as a priest of the Muses, I sing to virgin girls and boys songs never heard before.' Perhaps this poem of mine was creative in a new way. I had discovered myth and found new meaning in it, but I had not written myth until now. This was my own myth about my interior journey through depression. Reading it again after many months I am aware of many strands within it, but I am most pleased that the cat which began as a rather weak image in my last picture (see chapter 1) has become a lion caged and netted but struggling for his freedom. The battle is so costly that when he escapes he is not his former self, but he can develop a new life in freedom:

I am finding a new life
I know myself better
and so have more of myself to offer
Though I can do less

I can be more
I am open to new possibilities
I am discovering new enthusiasms
often growing in new forms from old roots
I am beginning to use my imagination
more fully and creatively
and in tandem with my intellect
I am learning how not to write
and sometimes how to write
I am testing out what I can do
and if progress is slow
it is nonetheless sure
I am forgetting to look back
even at real achievement
because what lies ahead is more exciting
I cannot control what may happen
and no longer feel I must
but I can trust to providence
which means
there is a saving possibility
in whatever we may face

What strikes me about this piece of writing is that much of it is in the present continuous tense: I am in the process of becoming myself. I cannot imagine a point at which I become myself, for that would imply a stasis which is incompatible with the developing, changing, journeying self that I am discovering. As I recover I am moving away from the edges over which I might fall back into the dark destructiveness of depression, though I know there still may be precipices to avoid. I have been travelling through a border country but now I am reaching a frontier which offers life in a new country, with a new language to learn and new challenges to face.

As I have journeyed into the depths of my being, I have been journeying towards God. The road which leads to becoming myself has converged with the road which guides me towards the mystery of God. The more I become myself, the better I know God. Finding the way has often been a struggle and like Jacob I have wrestled with a stranger whom only later I recognised as God (Genesis 32.22-32). Like Jacob I am limping as I continue my journey but because I have met with God I live more at ease with the self that I am becoming. I accept the light and dark within me because God loves me as I am. As I learn more of what I want with the whole of my being, I am discerning what God's will for me may be and I trust that the whispering wisdom that arises from within may be the prompting of the Spirit:

The Spirit of love and truth
flies free
allowing us to soar
as a seagull
to explore the heights and depths
of human experience
and to follow where the Spirit leads

POSTSCRIPT

As in May 1993 I wrote the last paragraph of chapter 16, I thought this book was as finished as it could be, but there was a final test for me to undergo. In chapter 10 we left my mother ill in the nursing home, expecting her to die reasonably soon. Unexpectedly my brother John became seriously ill in June and he died within six weeks. I was shattered:

The days are dead
and I am numb
unfeeling even
until assaulted by torrents
of unreasoning panic
and unreasoned anxiety
while in my dreams
I cry for you

Now that you are gone
I feel burdened again
not by any duty
you have laid upon me
nor by any business
you have left undone

Such was not your way
I struggle once more
with the tattered history
of our sick family
from which you gained a measure
of sane independence
It is as if I am left
alone
to heal its broken remains
Without you
I lack strength and resolve

Oh dear! I thought I had given up being the family problem-solver. The shock of grief often causes regressions like this, and we need not worry about them, so long as we understand what is happening. I went on:

The cancer that killed you
is the same cancer
that haunted my childhood years
It still has the power
unreasonably to terrify
though perhaps I recognise
sooner than before
where lies the source of my fear
Your going reminds me
of the brokenness of my life
and the inevitability of its end
Three down
and three to go
one nearing her end
another almost willing it

and me
fighting for life
and battling with fear

Only perfect love casts out fear
and the more love I give and receive
the less will be the grip of fear
or so I trust
In those last six weeks
did you come to such a trust?
Did you maintain it
in the face of death?
And will I?

John's death seemed to remove my mother's will to live and with the onset of autumn she began to fade away. As we began to talk of what must be, I became aware that her dying was an acute crisis for me. My relationship with her was still complicated by unhappy events and ambivalent emotions and I felt I had to sort out my feelings and forgive her before she died. The feelings were very strong and often contradictory and for a long time I was almost unable to talk to her. I did my best but it wasn't very good and I wondered how much of my ambivalence communicated itself to her. Then a few days before her death I was taking part in a Julian meeting. Quite unexpectedly in the silence I was filled with an assurance that I had truly forgiven her. She was beyond telling, but this is part of what I wrote:

The candle flickers
the flame sinking into the wax
The silence gathers
deepens into contemplation
Both speak of your departing

I have little to say to you
old lady who is my mother no more
You are
unexpectedly
resigned to the waiting time
at ease with what must come
Perhaps
after all your worries
you have found your salvation
All I can give that you need
is my kiss
Yet before you go
I forgive the other you
the younger you who lives in me
still
I forgive you
for failing to care for me
as a mother should
I forgive you
for abusing me
as no mother should

I can hear your protest
I never abused you
Whatever you did left me
confused
imprisoned
frozen
in a state of tension
from which I could not escape
until now
for I forgive you

and I am healed
The kiss I give you
says I love you
just before it is too late

So her funeral was an occasion when I could feel sad but say an honest heartfelt goodbye, when the death of the old lady did not raise ghosts of the younger mother that I had internalised as a child, when death became a healing for her ills and for my muddle and fear. I felt God's presence at that funeral as never before and I think others felt as I did.

Looking back from the funeral I can see more clearly how the God with whom I wrestled so long in depression was with me in the depths. God was in the rage that boiled up from within. Perhaps God was in the questions I kept asking of those I saw as modern scribes and pharisees: Matthew 23 is such a satifying chapter! God was in the guilt that accused me of failing my sister and pushed me towards self-destruction, bearing it for me, holding out hands to pull me back from the brink. God was in the pain with me, leading me like the Good Shepherd, holding me safe in the hollow of such tender hands. God was in my grief, encouraging my tears and bringing my sadness through to joy. God was and is the love that heals my broken relationships. How do I know? I have felt it as gift and grace from the hands and hearts of those who have brought me through to the knowledge that Dylan Thomas put so well:

Though lovers be lost love shall not
And death shall have no more dominion

ACKNOWLEDGEMENTS

The writing which gave rise to this book originated in many hours of discussion and therapy with Roger Burford, Jean Clark and Bill Hughes. The response when Trust published my poem about being on the edge of the church in September 1991 suggested that what I was struggling to say might be welcomed by a wider audience. I am grateful to Glennis Foote and Elizabeth Gregory-Smith for their thoughtful comments on some of my early writing; to Maurice Burrell and the Diocesan Training Team who gave me the chance to develop my ideas further alongside Jean, Bill and Margaret in clergy workshops in 1992-3; to Alan Webster, for his encouraging and perceptive comments on the first draft; and to Hilary Wakeman whose invitation to give two Colegate Seminars in 1993-4 encouraged the reflection which gave final form to this book.

Books that offered me a lifeline when depressed are listed in the bibliography, which contains details of all the books mentioned in the text. I owe a real debt to each of them. I have tried to attribute key ideas to their authors in the text, but some have escaped. I owe 'we are not responsible for the emotions that arise within us, but we are responsible for what we do with them' to Hugh Buckingham in *Feeling Good,* and 'God is in it with us' to Adrian Plass in *The Growing Up Pains of Adrian Plass. Feeling Good* (a coincidental title) by David Burns (Signet 1981) introduced me to cognitive therapy and especially to the technique of talking back to the feelings that distressed me, but I have not included it in the bibliography: it is a book to read when you are well! Reading and re-reading many of the books has made them so much a part of my thinking that I may be guilty of unconscious plagiarism: if that is so, I apologise.

Special thanks are due to Teresa Hawkins, for sharing her son Daniel with us and allowing me to write so freely about him; to Judith Price, for the painful sharing which led to the poem addressed to her and for permission to use it in chapter 16; to Jessica Aidley, for the sculpture which enabled me to pray in the darkness; to Roger, Jean and Bill, for their loving care in this latest depression; to my daughters Lisa and Anna, who have lived through three of my depressions with me, and most of all to my wife Margaret, who has lived through all five. Without her love, perception, tolerance and courage I could not have undertaken the journey that I have attempted to describe and this book would not have been written.

Peter Brice   Mundesley, October 1994

BIBLIOGRAPHY

The first list contains books which helped me to hold on in the depths of depression. All of them have short sections which suit the poor concentration common in depression.

BASSET E   *Love in my Meaning*   DLT 1973
                        A comforting anthology for times of sadness

CARTER S   *Dance in the Dark*   Fount 1980
                        For times when it is hard to believe

COTTER J   *Prayer at Night*   Cairns Publications 1983
                        Cairns for a Journey is a guide to the dark

De MELLO A   *The Prayer of the Frog*   Prakash (India) 1988
                        Stories to carry in the mind and ponder

ELIOT T S   *Complete Poems and Plays*   Faber & Faber 1969
                        The *Four Quartets* have much to say, especially 'be
                        still, and let the dark come upon you'

GIBRAN K   *The Prophet*   1926, Heinemann 1972
                        Profound wisdom to be treasured and pondered

HAMMARSKJOLD D *Markings*   Faber & Faber 1964
                        The journal of the Swedish UN Secretary-General

| HEANEY S & HUGHES T | *The Rattle Bag* | Faber & Faber 1982 |

HEANEY S   *The Rattle Bag*   Faber & Faber 1982
HUGHES T   An exciting and varied anthology of poetry

KOSSOFF D   *A Small Town is a World*   Robson 1979, Pan 1980
Witty and wise short stories about Rabbi Mark

KOSSOFF D   *You have a minute, Lord?*   Robson 1977, Pan 1978
A way forward when praying is difficult

QUOIST M   *With Open Heart*   Gill & Macmillan 1983
More wisdom from this French Catholic priest

ROBINSON J A T   *The Roots of a Radical*   SCM 1981
For the meditations in chapter 9

ROBINSON J A T   *Where Three Ways Meet*   SCM 1987
For the sermons in chapter 10

SYKES W G D   *Visions of Faith*   Marshall Pickering 1986
The introduction spells out ways of using this anthology of reflections.

SYKES W G D   *Visions of Love*   Bible Reading Fellowship 1992
The first of three anthologies of reflections growing out of *Visions of Faith*

WHITAKER A   *All in the End is Harvest*   DLT/CRUSE 1984
An anthology for those who grieve

The second list is of passages from the Bible which became important to me. I would use a breathing exercise to relax my body and mind and then read the passage slowly several times, close my eyes and ponder what I had read. I learned to jot down any phrase that struck me and any thoughts that it stimulated.

Genesis 32.23-32   Wrestling with God

2 Samuel 1.19-27   David's lament for Saul and Jonathan

Psalms 23, 91, 121	Comfort and protection
Psalm 51	A confession
Psalm 88	A prayer from the depths
Psalm 103	God forgives
Psalm 139.11-12	God is in the dark as much as the light
Ecclesiastes 3.1-8	Wait for the right time – no targets!
Isaiah 43.18-20	A new beginning is always possible
Isaiah 55	God's invitation
Matthew 4.1-11	Facing temptation in the wilderness
Matthew 5.3-12	'Blessed are you....'
Matthew 6.25-34	'Be not anxious...'
Matthew 23.13-33	It's all right to be angry!
Mark 5.1-20	Imagine the pigs carrying away the feelings that torment
Luke 7.36-50	Even great sins can be forgiven
Luke 15.11-31	The good news is that God loves us, whoever we are, whatever we have done
John 7.53-8.11	'Neither do I condemn you'
Romans 8.31-39	Nothing separates us from God's love
1 Corinthians 13-14.1	'Make love your aim'
Galatians 5.22-23	The harvest of the Spirit
James 3.17	The wisdom from above
1 John 4.7-21	'God is love'

The third list contains books which helped me to wrestle with the darkness and the God I found there.

BLY R   *Iron John*   Element 1991
                         How myths may heal our wounds

BUCKINGHAM H   *Feeling Good*   Epworth 1989
                         Coping without guilt with our chaotic emotions

BRYANT C   *Jung and the Christian Way*   DLT 1983
                         An interpretation of Jung for Christians

DEWAR F   *Live for a Change*   DLT 1988
                         A guide to discovering our gifts

DODD C H   *The Founder of Christianity*   Collins 1971
                         A fine portrait of the historical Jesus

DOMINIAN J   *The Capacity to Love*   DLT 1985
                         What love is and how it may transform people

HUGHES G W   *God of Surprises*   DLT 1985
                         A splendid guide to our inner journey

KUBLER-ROSS E   *On Death and Dying*   Tavistock 1970
                         Facing our own mortality

MACKEY J P   *Jesus: the Man and the Myth*   SCM 1979
                         Myth as a way of conveying truth about Jesus

MAYNE M   *A Year Lost and Found*   DLT 1987
                         Both a diary of a year suffering from ME and a
                         reflection on suffering, redemption and hope

MITCHELL S   *The Gospel According to Jesus*   Rider 1992
                         The good news as taught by Jesus

MORLEY J   *All Desires Known*   MOW/WIT 1988, SPCK 1992
                         New ways of addressing God in prayer

MULLEN P   *Being Saved*   SCM 1985
This illuminating book argues that spirituality and
psychology are two sides of the same coin.

PALMER M   *Living Christianity*   Element 1993
Changing the way we tell the Christian story

PECK M S   *The Road Less Travelled*   Hutchinson 1983
A psychiatrist explores love and spirituality

PLASS A   *The Growing up Pains*   Marshall Pickering 1989
                  of Adrian Plass
The story of how he came to feel loved

SHEPPARD G   *An Aspect of Fear*   DLT 1989
Overcoming the disabling effects of fear

SKINNER R   *Families and how to survive them*   Methuen 1983
& CLEESE J   Commonsense about family relationships

STETTBACHER K   *Making Sense of Suffering*   Dutton 1991
Therapy that heals the wounds of childhood

STEVENS A   *On Jung*   Routledge 1990, Penguin 1991
A good introduction to his life and thought

TILBY A   *Won't You Join the Dance?*   SPCK 1985
A creative way of looking at the creeds

VERMES G   *Jesus the Jew*   SCM 1973, 1983
A Jewish scholar examines the Jesus of history

WICKES F G   *The Inner World of Choice*   Coventure 1977
A challenge to find our life's inner meaning and
mystery, so that we make our own choices.

WILLIAMS H A   *The True Wilderness*   Constable 1965
Belief expounded with simplicity and sincerity

WREN B *What Language Shall I Borrow?* SCM 1989
Finding new ways of naming God

YOUNG F *Face to Face* T & T Clark 1990
Subtitled *a narrative essay in the theology of suffering,* its honesty compels attention.